RAILS TO THE COAST
East Anglian Seaside Stations, Sheds and Rail Links
Great Yarmouth and Lowestoft

By
Malcolm R. White
Coastal and Maritime Heritage Series
2004

INFORMATION

Published by Malcolm R. White
Coastal Publications
71 Beeching Drive
Lowestoft
NR32 4TB
First Published June 2004

Printed by Micropress Printers Ltd.
27 Norwich Road
Halesworth
Suffolk
IP19 8BX
ISBN 09547323 0 8

Every effort has been made to ensure the information contained in this review is accurate and for this reason many sources of information have been consulted. These include personal accounts of events, official documentation, local diaries, media resources, and numerous accredited research works. However, when considering such a complex, varied and historical subject, 100% accuracy cannot be guaranteed. By popular request, all measurements, dimensions and distances in this book are stated in British Imperial. Books in this series are part of the National Published Archive, and as such are included in the library collections of the British Library, the National Library of Scotland, the National Library of Wales, the Universities of Oxford and Cambridge, Trinity College, Dublin, and when appropriate, The National Museum of Science & Industry. Unlike the majority of publications, this book is not produced for commercial gain for the author or publisher, profits from the series are donated to railway charities and good causes.

OTHER TITLES IN THE UNIQUE COASTAL AND MARITIME HERITAGE SERIES

DOWN THE HARBOUR 1955-1995	40 years of fishing vessels, owners, the harbour and shipyards at Lowestoft	ISBN 09532485 0X
A CENTURY OF FISHING	Fishing from Great Yarmouth and Lowestoft 1899-1999	ISBN 09532485 18
FISHING WITH DIVERSITY	A portrait of the Colne Group of Lowestoft	ISBN 09532485 26
CROWNIES OF LOWESTOFT	The steam trawler fleet of Consolidated Fisheries	ISBN 09532485 34
DRIFTING, TRAWLING & SHIPPING	A portrait of Small & Co. (Lowestoft) Ltd.	ISBN 09532485 42
GREETINGS FROM LOWESTOFT	A picture book of old postcards and photographs	ISBN 09532485 50
THE LOWESTOFT TRAIN	The railway at Lowestoft and scenes on the lines to Norwich, Ipswich and Yarmouth	ISBN 09532485 69
LOWESTOFT ANTIQUITY	A picture book of once familiar scenes	ISBN 09532485 77
THE BOSTON PUTFORD STORY (1)	Fishing and Offshore Support from Great Yarmouth and Lowestoft	ISBN 09532485 85
LOWESTOFT CORPORATION TRANSPORT	Lowestoft Trams, Buses and Bygone Town Scenes	ISBN 09532485 93

PHOTOGRAPHS

Front Cover (Top) - In the days when newspapers were distributed overnight by rail, the newspaper vans were often taken to Lowestoft by Class 47 Co-Co locomotives. On 3rd April 1987, No. 47487 of Stratford depot , a Class 47/4, complete with the cockney sparrow on the sides, is see in Platform Four. A Class 101 Metro-Cammell DMU is in Platform Three and the sadly missed overall station roof, removed in 1992, can be seen. (NF)

Front Cover (Bottom) - Britannia Class 7MT 4-6-2 No. 70002 *Geoffrey Chaucer* of Stratford shed, waits at London Liverpool Street for the next trip to Norwich. These locomotives were expected to make two double trips to Norwich, 460 miles in all, each day. Two of this class are preserved. (DWC)

Title Page - Gresley designed B17/6 4-6-0 No. 61609 *Quidenham* passes Woodbridge with a mid day van train in the early 1950s. This superb scene, complete with a fine display of road vehicles, was recorded from the footbridge at the station. (JH/EMJ)

Opposite Page - Britannia Class 7MT 4-6-2 No. 70012 *John Of Gaunt* of Norwich shed, passes Shenfield with a down express on the 1st August 1960. Steam haulage on passenger services between London and Norwich officially ended in September 1961. (FC)

CONTENTS

ACKNOWLEDGEMENTS

Much appreciated has been the cooperation and support offered during the preparation of this book by several kind people interested in researching and recording local railway history, and the many dedicated railway enthusiasts who have offered the use of their photographic collections for use in this book. These include in particular, Mr. Stuart Jones BA, who has provided editorial support for the many titles in this popular series. Assisting or participating in this complex project have been Mr. Peter Calvert, Mr. Bryn Colton, Mr. Norman Fairhead, Mr. Alfred Hubbard, Mr. Peter Killby, Mr. Geoffrey Moore, Mr. Peter Parker, Mr. Ronnie Paul, Mr. Terry Reeve, Mr. Peter Snell, Mr. David White, Mr. Steffan White and Louise Clarke and the very helpful staff of the Lowestoft Record Office. Last but not least, I would like to thank my wife, Cathryn, for the patience, support and understanding she has shown during the very long hours I spend writing, publishing and distributing books in this series.

PHOTOGRAPHIC OWNERSHIP AND COPYRIGHT

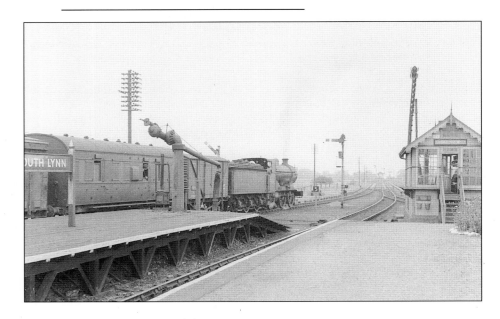

On the former Midland & Great Northern Railway, South Lynn was considered the gateway to East Anglia. At the western end of the station, Class J6 0-6-0 No. 64176, a H. N. Gresley and H. A. Ivatt Great Northern design, introduced in 1911, leaves with a van train. This locomotive, one of 110 built, was for many years allocated to New England (35A) shed. (*FC*)

INTRODUCTION

Today, the railway lines to the seaside locations of Felixstowe, Lowestoft, Great Yarmouth, Cromer and Sheringham represent only half of those Norfolk and Suffolk coastal towns previously served by rail, with Southwold, Aldeburgh, Mundesley, Wells and Hunstanton no longer found on the railway network map of the British Isles. Most of the resorts originally served by rail relied heavily upon the holiday trade for their existence, and indeed some only saw substantial growth after the coming of the railway. It was the railway that gave the great majority of the British population the chance to sample the delights of the east coast and the attractive seaside towns situated thereon. The area was well served by the Great Eastern Railway (GER) and the Midland & Great Northern Joint Railway (M&GNJR), both concerns consisting of a combination of a number of smaller companies. Two coastal routes were provided by a joint committee comprising the GER and M&GN, and a third, much loved by locals, by the Southwold Railway Company.

These important coastal rail links also allowed East Coast towns with a fishing industry to dispatch vast qualities of fresh fish and shellfish to inland markets, towns and cities. Items such as coal, wood, bricks, and salt, previous carried by ship, could be delivered quicker to the coastal resorts and ports by the railway. Due to the advent of the motor car and coach and the availability of cheap foreign package holidays, passenger numbers declined on the lines to the east coast. In some cases the services became uneconomic and were withdrawn, resulting in passenger services to Lowestoft, Great Yarmouth, Felixstowe, Cromer and Sheringham remaining today.

At the time of writing (2004), freight services continue to Lowestoft with substantial quantities of products associated with the offshore gas and oil industry handled there.

The area's largest holiday resort, Great Yarmouth, where the first railway station at Vauxhall opened in 1844, has seen a major reduction in rail links, with two of the town's three stations, Beach and South Town, having closed. However, the town remains a major destination for large numbers of rail passengers who arrive there for their holidays. Lowestoft has been part of the railway network since 1847 and retains two routes out of the town, to Ipswich and Norwich. A third line, the direct route to Yarmouth via Gorleston, which opened in July 1903, closed in May 1970. Two earlier routes between Lowestoft and Yarmouth were via Reedham and the other via St. Olaves.

Both Lowestoft and Great Yarmouth have direct services to London throughout the year, with Lowestoft services travelling over the somewhat restrictive but vital East Suffolk Line and the Great Yarmouth services via Norwich.

In most cases, rail links to towns are increasingly seen as a major asset within the community, benefiting residents, the tourist industry, visitors to the area, the environment and the business community. However, it has been recorded in the local press that many residents and businesses who are principally road users, want the existing rail services substantially curtailed, especially at Lowestoft, or do not want a railway at all.

This book features scenes, and the principal stations and sheds on the main routes from London Liverpool Street, Peterborough and South Lynn to the east coast resorts of Great Yarmouth and Lowestoft. More information about railways in the Lowestoft and Yarmouth area can be found in another book in this series, "The Lowestoft Train", which was published in 2002.

Malcolm White
Lowestoft
June 2004

YARMOUTH BEACH
YARMOUTH SOUTH TOWN
YARMOUTH VAUXHALL

Clean rolling stock both internally and externally, is an important part of creating a good customer care culture and image for the railway operators of today and was also in the past, as shown here at Yarmouth Beach in the 1950s. After closure in 1959 the station area became the town's coach station. Unlike some station platforms in East Anglia today, this one was well cared for, with no litter, grass, or weeds to be seen. (*EDPpics*)

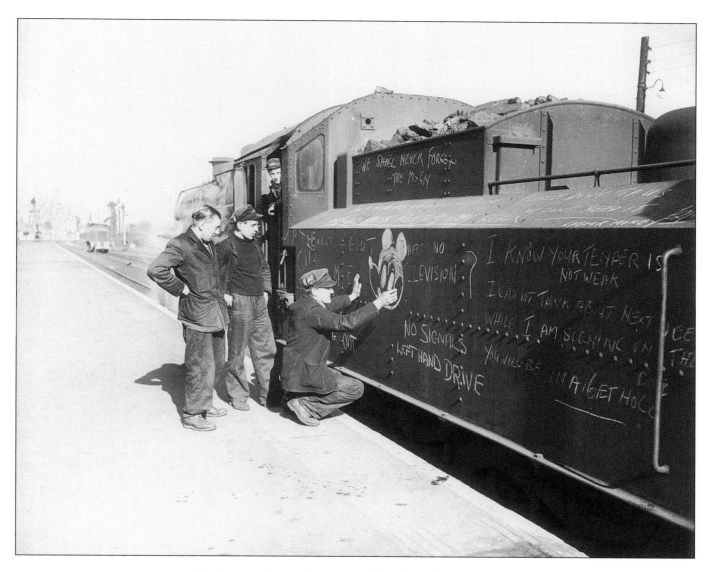

It came as no great surprise to many people that the closure of Yarmouth Beach and the railway to the midlands and the north took place in February 1959. The line had sustained declining traffic over many years, it was becoming increasingly expensive to maintain and in many cases similar services could be provided via Norwich. At one time providing a major route into East Anglia, the former M&GN main line was steam worked until the end. Designed by H. G. Ivatt for the L.M.S. and introduced in 1947, the Class 4MT 2-6-0s were, in the 1950s, very much the mainstay of the motive power used on services over this attractive line. With closure only hours away, the tender of this Class 4MT at Yarmouth Beach station is being adorned with slogans appropriate for the occasion. (*EDPpics*)

A once familiar scene at Yarmouth Beach showing one of the large class of M&GN Class C 4-4-0's on shed. This locomotive, No. 12, had been fitted with an extended firebox just prior to World War One and, when recorded on 15th May 1937, was fitted with a flowerpot chimney. Built in 1894 to a S. J. Johnson design, No. 12 was scrapped after service with the LNER in August 1942. (*MWC*)

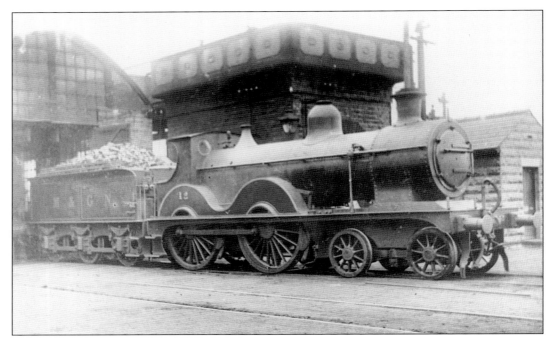

At Yarmouth Beach, M&GN Class D 0-6-0 No. 64 was well placed for the photographer to record this fine scene on 29th June 1914 . (*LCGB/KN*)

The M&GN took great pride in the cleanliness, presentation and general appearance of their locomotives and rolling stock. A fine example of which is the condition of M&GN Class A 4-4-0 No. 23, seen here at Yarmouth Beach, on 29th June 1914. (*LCGB/KN*)

The date is 9th July 1950, and amongst the locomotives on shed at Yarmouth Beach is S.D. Holden designed Class F6 2-4-2T No. 67223. For many years allocated to Beach shed, by the mid 1950s No. 67223 had moved on to Lowestoft.

Once the M&GN was incorporated into the LNER, the motive power and rolling stock was progressively brought into line with LNER practice. A wide range of former GER locomotive classes such as J65, J68, F5, J17, D16/3 and B12/3 appeared and dominated the scene. (*SLS*)

Visiting Yarmouth Beach station on a day in 1949 no doubt proved a memorable experience for the children of St. Georges Infants School. These unique scenes illustrate the day-to-day happenings at a busy station and provide details of the station and yard not normally seen in other railway publications. **Top left** - With Class B12/3 4-6-0 No. 61533. This locomotive spent many years shedded at Yarmouth Beach and was scrapped at Stratford in November 1959. **Top right** - With an unidentified Class F6 2-4-2T waiting in the platform. In the background is Yarmouth Yard Signal Box. **Bottom left and right** - With the same Class F6 and behind the children the platform and station. (DWC)

One of the many attractions that Yarmouth Beach could provide for the enthusiast in the mid 1950s was No. 68214, the sole remaining Class J65 0-6-0T locomotive. Twenty of these J. Holden designed light branch locomotives were built for the GER, and were designated Class E22. No. 68214 is seen here at Beach on 1st October 1955. (*LCGB/KN*)

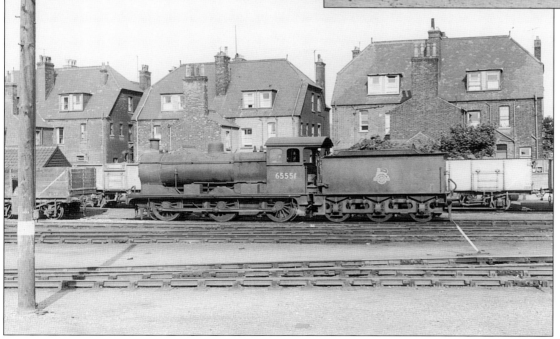

Moving on to 1958, we find a locomotive in the Beach station yard which was well known at that time on the eastern section of the former M&GN.
Melton Constable's Class J17 0-6-0 No. 65551 complete with tablet catcher, is seen resting on a glorious August day. (*FC*)

In 1955, Yarmouth Beach was the home shed of Class J68 0-6-0T No. 68651 where it is seen in the yard. The Class J68 were the largest Great Eastern 0-6-0T engines and in 1955, many were allocated to sheds in Norfolk and Suffolk. They were introduced in 1912, at a time when the Locomotive Superintendent of the Great Eastern Railway changed from S. Dewer Holden to A. J. Hill, and were a development of the Class J69 with side window cabs. (*SLS*)

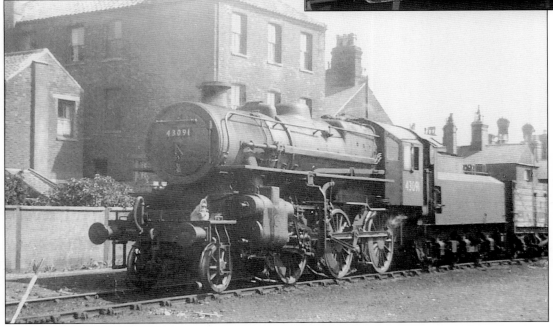

Another of the numerous Ivatt Class 4MTs, No. 43091, in the yard at Beach station and bathed in summer sunshine. The date is 10th July 1955 and at the time, this engine was allocated to South Lynn. Prior to the closure of the Breydon Viaduct in 1953, these engines could often be found working the 11.15am Yarmouth Beach - Lowestoft train and the 12.33pm return. On 16th April 1952, it is recorded that No. 43091 was in charge of these trains. (*NF*)

After leaving the Norfolk & Suffolk Joint Line at North Gorleston Junction, trains from Lowestoft to Yarmouth Beach ventured on to a M&GN built section of line known as the Lowestoft Junction Railway, a major feature of which was Breydon Viaduct. **Below** - The general view of the Viaduct from the north bank. *(MWC)*
Bottom - An unusual view of the Viaduct showing it open for river traffic.
In the back ground on the left can be seen Yarmouth Vauxhall carriage sidings, and on the right, the engine shed. The bridge was dismantled in 1962, having closed to passenger trains in 1953. It cost £67,628-2s-4d to build. *(LCGB/KN)*

Above - After crossing a number of other bridges, these fine signals were passed on the approach to Nelson Road level crossing and Yarmouth Beach. *(MWC)*.

Connecting Yarmouth Beach and the quayside tramway of the GER, the Yarmouth Union gave the M&GN and its predecessors access to the requirements and custom of the important fishing industry and allowed the transferring of wagons between the GER and M&GN. A coal depot was set up on this section of track which remained in use until 1970, with access being gained from Vauxhall after closure of the M&GN. The Yarmouth Union Railway opened on 15th May 1882 and a new junction was installed with the opening in 1903 of the Lowestoft line. This view of part of the Yarmouth Union Railway was recorded on 28th February 1959. (MW)

Yarmouth Beach station (MW)
Left and Right - Platform detail

Above - Although regarded by some people as ugly, the Ivatt 4MT 2-6-0 locomotives proved to be economical, reliable and well suited for working the former M &GN lines. Today they would be an ideal choice for many of today's heritage railways, however only one now remains of the 162 built, and this is normally to be found on the Severn Valley Railway. Introduced by the LMS in 1947, this mixed traffic type was designed by H. G. Ivatt. One of the class, No. 43157,is seen at Yarmouth Beach shed where it was allocated for many years. This type of locomotive symbolised the former M&GN in the last few years of its existence. (*RAS*)

Demolition of Yarmouth Beach (32F)
Yarmouth Beach engine shed and associated structures were quickly removed.
Top Right - An intact shed and turntable on 28th February 1959. (*MW*)
Centre Right - The same location on 14th March 1959. (*MW*)
Bottom Right - Almost the same location on 30th April 1959. (*MW*)

By June 1959, the station area and yard had been totally cleared of all track, signalling, and fittings, with only the main buildings remaining. A diesel shunter had been employed in the demolition work.

After closure the buildings remained intact and many former railway facilities such as left luggage, toilets, refreshment room, waiting room and the booking hall continued in use as a coach station.

Above - The goods shed and end of the main platform. (*MW*)
Left - Part of the main building showing entrance to the booking hall. (*MW*)

Yarmouth South Town was another station the town could be proud of. However, after losing the London services and finally becoming an unmanned station serving only the Lowestoft line, the parts of the building still in railway use became somewhat untidy and vandalised. This superb scene from the 1950s of a clean, well kept and tidy station will bring back happy memories to a great many people, including the author who used the station a great deal. After becoming unmanned, much of this building was used for offices and a depot by Santa Fe (UK) Ltd., a company involved in offshore oil and gas exploration. In 1966, Yarmouth South Town was the destination for hundreds of tons of heavy freight in the form of pipes used in offshore work, these trains travelling to South Town via Lowestoft and the coast line. Whilst most of the London services were diverted to Vauxhall station, some summer holiday expresses from London Liverpool Street terminated at South Town as late as 1966. The station finally closed on 4th May 1970 together with the railway to Lowestoft, and no trace of this fine large building exists today. (*EDPpics*)

GER Class G16 4-4-0 No 0704 at Yarmouth South Town. All of this class, built originally as compounds, had been withdrawn by 1904. Some parts of these locomotives were later used on Class T19 engines. The Class G16, built in 1884-85, were considered to have an advanced appearance for their time. (*LCGB/KN*)

A scene at Yarmouth on 12th July 1901 showing GER 0-4-2T No. 145 waiting in the station sidings. (*LCGB/KN*)

LNER "Super-Claud" Class D16/2 4-4-0 No. 8822 was recorded on shed at Yarmouth South Town in October 1932. This locomotive was later rebuilt to Class D16/3 and renumbered No. 7692 in 1942, No. 2573 in 1946 and finally No. 62573 in 1949. Entering service with the Great Eastern Railway in October 1909, No. 62573 was withdrawn from traffic at Kings Lynn, and scrapped at Stratford in October 1955. (RAS)

LNER Class D15 4-4-0 No. 8854 on shed at
Yarmouth South Town in the 1930s. Later
rebuilt to Class D16/3, and renumbered No.
2545 in 1946 and No. 62545 in 1949, this
locomotive was withdrawn from service in
September 1958. (*RAS*)

Yarmouth South Town as many will
remember it, clean, orderly and well kept.
Nicely presented coaching stock of a London
Liverpool Street train, complete with full
restaurant car, can be seen on the
right. (*StationsUK*)

Class B17/4 4-6-0 No. 61664 *Liverpool* backs down from the sheds at South Town in preparation to take out a London Liverpool Street service on 30th July 1958. In the distance can be seen the sheds (32D), and on the left are trucks carrying insulated containers for the conveyance of products from the local Birds Eye factory. (*FC*)

Class D16/3 4-4-0 No. 62604, a long time South Town engine, leaves the station with a local train. The cleanliness of the coaches of the Yarmouth South Town to London Liverpool Street train on the right is most impressive and matches the general appearance of the station. No. 62604 was one of the 1933 Gresley rebuilds of the Class D15 locomotives. The D15s were themselves a development of the original J. Holden "Claud Hamilton" Class. (*FC*)

Having worked in from Lowestoft, Class F6 2-4-2T No. 67229 waits in the sidings at Yarmouth South Town to take the next train back. With the other Holden designed 2-4-2T locomotives these engines were a common sight at Lowestoft and Great Yarmouth for many years. No. 67229 was one of the last two of this type to be shedded locally, the other was No. 67231, both were withdrawn in March 1958. (DW)

During the 1950s, two push-pull fitted S. D. Holden designed Class F5 2-4-2T engines were allocated to Yarmouth South Town for use on local services to Lowestoft and on the East Suffolk line. The two, No. 67199 and 67218, were fitted for push-pull working in 1949 and No. 67218 is seen here on shed at South Town. (PT)

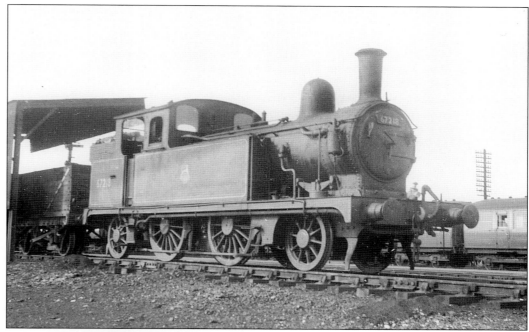

Push-pull operation was a common mode of working on the coast line between Yarmouth and Lowestoft and also on the East Suffolk line from Yarmouth South Town. Types of locomotives used in the last years of steam operation were Classes F5, C12 and N7.

This view shows a train, propelled by a Class N7 0-6-2T, approaching Yarmouth South Town. The embankment, which until 1953 carried the line from Gorleston North Junction to Yarmouth Beach, is just visible though the steam coming from the engine. (DW)

After closure of the Yarmouth South Town to Beccles line in 1959, the services to London ran via Lowestoft. However, after a relatively short period, these were diverted to Yarmouth Vauxhall running via Norwich to London. This left South Town with only the service to Lowestoft remaining. On 2nd May 1970 this too was withdrawn with the result that Yarmouth South Town closed completely. Much of the land seen here was quickly purchased and is now in use as a dual carriageway road and retail park. Specialised freight services continued to South Town via Lowestoft until 1966.

Above - A Derby lightweight diesel multiple unit arrives at Yarmouth South Town in the late 1950s. (MWC)
Left - In the later years of steam operation on the line between Lowestoft and Great Yarmouth, Class N7 0-6-2 tank engines replaced the various types of older 2-4-2 and 4-4-2 tank engines previously used. One of these N7s was N7/2 No. 69690 seen here at Yarmouth South Town. Introduced in 1926, as a development of the N7/1, the N7/2 had long travel valves. Seen displaying a Cambridge (31A) shed plate, No. 69690 was transferred to Lowestoft from there in July 1958, shortly after which this scene was recorded. (FC)

It is August 1958 and Class B17/6 4-6-0 No. 61636 *Harlaxton Manor* arrives at Yarmouth Vauxhall. The bridge under which the engine has just passed is one of those that carried the former M&GN line from Gorleston North Junction to Yarmouth Beach station. The line closed to passengers in 1953 and during March 1959 the track was recovered. (FC)

From Vauxhall goods yard, a 1¾ mile street tramway existed which provided rail access to the once very busy fish market. In more recent times it allowed the frozen food producer Birds Eye to move vast amounts of their products away from their Yarmouth factory by rail. A variety of locomotives were used on the tramway including a Sentinel, Classes J65 and J70, and diesel mechanical shunters such as Gardner powered 0-6-0 No. 11103, seen here shunting in the yard at Vauxhall on 7th August 1958, complete with guards fitted for working over the tramway some of which was on public roads. (*FC*)

Another fine view of No. 11103 at Vauxhall, displaying a well placed 32E (Vauxhall) shedplate. These locomotives were introduced in 1952 and were later designated Class O4. The street tramway, over which this and small steam locomotives worked, saw a dramatic fall in traffic with the demise of the fishing industry at Yarmouth, which by 1963 had collapsed. During the last years of operation this valuable rail link carried vast quantities of scrap metal to A. King's scrapyard for export. Officially closed in 1976, the great majority of the tramway has now been recovered and little remains of this once important access to the industrial riverside premises of Great Yarmouth. (FC)

After leaving the station yard at Vauxhall access to the quayside lines and tramway at Great Yarmouth was over a bridge crossing the River Bure. LNER Class J65 0-6-0T No. 8215 was recorded having just crossed the bridge on 1st September 1948. The Class J65 was designed by J. Holden and introduced by the GER in 1889 as the Class E22. (LCGB/KN)

With the bridge carrying the line from Lowestoft to Yarmouth Beach in the background, Class D16/3 4-4-0 No. 62541 waits at Vauxhall on 9th July 1951 to work a return train to Norwich. (*SLS*)

In the 1950s Class V3 2-6-2T locomotives were uncommon on the lines of East Anglia. However on 9th July 1950, one of the class, No. 67679, was on shed at Yarmouth Vauxhall. This type of locomotive was normally to be found working in Scotland or the north east of England. The Class V3, introduced in 1939, was a development of the V1 with higher boiler pressure. (*SLS*)

Prior to the arrival, in the early 1950s, of a diesel shunter at Vauxhall for use along the quay tramway, the locomotives included Class J70 0-6-0T locomotives or "Tram Locos". Inside the shed at Vauxhall in 1932 we find LNER No. 7138, together with on the right, a double ended Sentinel Wagon Works designed locomotive, LNER No. 8403, also used on the tramway. (RAS)

Another of the "Tram Locos", LNER No. 7137 was also present. The motion was fully enclosed for working over public roads in Yarmouth.
Designed by J. Holden and introduced in 1903, these locomotives had Walschaerts valve gear, weighed just over 27 tons and had a tractive effort of 8,930 lbs. A similar "Tram Loco" was designed by T. W. Worsdell with a 0-4-0 wheel arrangement, and entered service in 1883. (RAS)

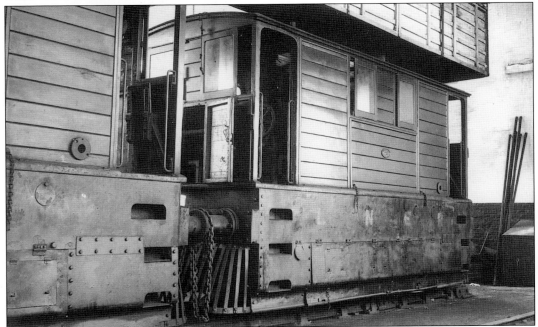

With a tractive effort of 32,080 lb Thompson designed Class L1 2-6-4T locomotives such as No. 67736, seen here at Vauxhall shed on 18th May 1958, were handy for working heavy summer extras in addition to local and goods trains. Prior to being based in East Anglia. No. 67736 was a Stratford locomotive and used on suburban work out of London Liverpool Street. In the background is the embankment which, until 1953, carried trains between Yarmouth Beach station and Lowestoft. It is now the location of a Great Yarmouth relief road. The site of the shed and yard are now occupied by a large ASDA supermarket and car park. (RAS)

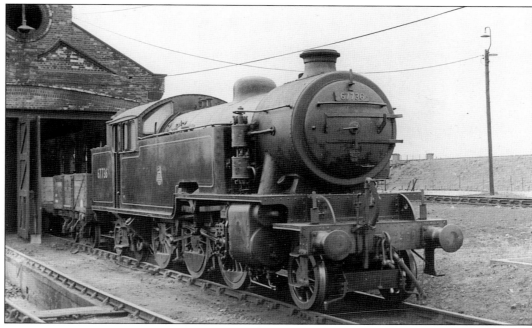

Introduced in 1961, the Class 25 Bo-Bo diesel electric locomotives were a common sight in the eastern counties, especially when hauling the summer trains to Great Yarmouth from the Midlands. After removal of the coaching stock by the resident Class 03 diesel shunter, Class 25/2 No. 25134 and Class 25/3 No. 25278 wait to reverse out of the platform at Yarmouth Vauxhall. Built by British Railways, with a Sulzer 6cyl 6LDA28-B 1250hp engine, this class became widely scattered and was initially allocated to all regions except the Southern and Western. (RF)

The stations at Great Yarmouth were always very busy on summer Saturdays, with many trains bringing holidaymakers to the resort. The rapid clearance of coaching stock from the platforms to the carriage sidings was undertaken in the diesel era by various types of diesel shunter including the Class 03. A member of this 204 hp 0-6-0 diesel mechanical class, No. 03180, is seen here at Yarmouth Vauxhall. Previously No. 03180 was numbered D2180. (*RF*)

The height of the holiday season at Great Yarmouth and at Vauxhall station three hauled trains, having arrived earlier full of holidaymakers, are waiting to depart. Two are headed by Class 31 A1A-A1A diesel electric locomotives, a type powered by an English Electric 12cyl 12SVT 1470hp engine giving a maximum speed of 90 mph, through four Brush TM73-68 traction motors. (*RF*)

With the present British policy of buying new diesel electric locomotives from overseas, many railway enthusiasts long to see scenes such as this. Class 37/0 Co-Co diesel electric locomotives No. 37057 and 37107 are seen together at Great Yarmouth on 1st July 1989 waiting to leave the resort with a summer through train to London. With dwindling numbers of these locomotives in service, the few members of this class that are seen in East Anglia are usually employed on special workings. Built by English Electric between 1960-65, this type is powered by an English Electric 12cyl 12CSVT 1750bhp diesel engine driving an English Electric Type 822/10G generator, which supplies power to six English Electric EE 538A traction motors, giving a maximum rated speed of 80mph. Both these locomotives are from Stratford depot and in 1989 were assigned for freightliner work. The Class 37 is considered by some as one of the most successful British diesel locomotive designs and at the time of writing (2004), are still used on front line passenger work in some parts of the UK. (NF)

Another Class 31 diesel locomotive, No. 31177 waits at the platform end at Vauxhall having arrived earlier with a Saturdays only summer train. This scene was recorded after the embankment built for the Lowestoft-Yarmouth Beach line had been removed, and before the Yarmouth relief road and bridge were constructed. Just visible in the distance are Vauxhall carriage sidings. (*NF*)

Through trains from London Liverpool Street consisting of hauled stock still run to Great Yarmouth, with Class 47 diesel electric locomotives being used for the part of the journey between Norwich and Yarmouth. Between Norwich and London electric traction is used, and on occasion the dead electric locomotive makes the trip to Great Yarmouth with the coaching stock. On 25th September 1993, Intercity Sector locomotive Class 86/2 Bo-Bo No. 86221 *BBC Look East* was at the seaside. The hauled stock of a cross country service is in the adjacent platform. (*MW*)

LOWESTOFT CENTRAL

One of the numerous Lowestoft based GER Holden designed 2-4-2T locomotives leaves the town for Beccles on an overcast day in May 1951. This Class F5, a rebuild of earlier F4 engines, is seen passing Lowestoft engine shed. The Class F5 was introduced during 1911. (*MWC*)

A finely detailed view of GER 2-4-0 No. 34, at Lowestoft on 9th July 1901. Built in 1869 by Sharp Stewart, the locomotive is standing in the sidings adjacent to Denmark Road in what is now the station car park.
No. 34 was one of 30 locomotives of this type built by Sharp Stewart, another ten were built by the Great Eastern Railway at Stratford. All had been withdrawn by the end of 1913.(*LCGB/KN*)

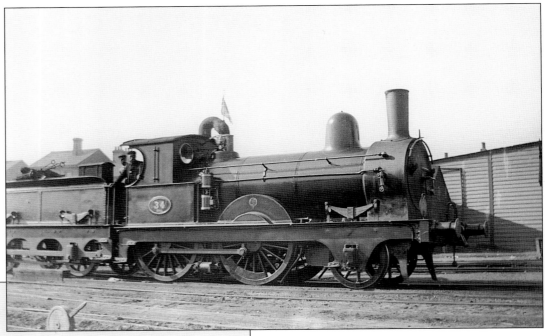

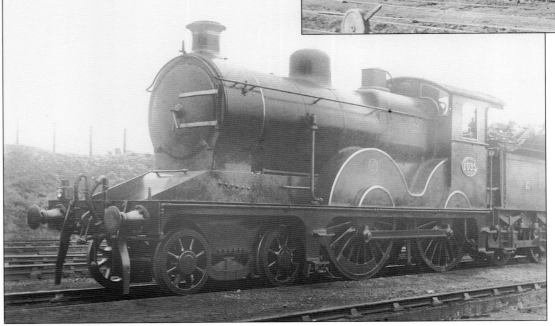

Great Eastern Railway rebuilt Class T19 4-4-0 No. 1035 on shed at Lowestoft on 3rd July 1914. Built in 1897, this locomotive was reclassified as a Class D13 by the LNER and was scrapped in 1943. It was the first of 60 to be rebuilt during 1905-08 from the original GER Class T19 "Standard" 2-4-0s, of which 110 were originally built. Twenty one others were rebuilt as "Humpty Dumpties" during 1902-04, whilst others were scrapped in their original condition before 1914. (*LCGB/KN*)

A superb Lowestoft scene at Coke Ovens Junction, as M&GN Class A 4-4-0 No. 34 gains the Norfolk & Suffolk Joint Railways Committee line to Yarmouth on 18th September 1926 and starts the climb to the first intermediate station, Lowestoft North. (*MWC*)

A nice view of M&GN Class A 4-4-0 No. 23 at Lowestoft Central waiting to depart with a train for Yarmouth Beach on 4th July 1914. The one time goods shed and yard on the north side of the station can be seen on the left. (*LCGB/KN*)

Much has changed at Lowestoft Central station since this scene was recorded in the 1960s. Today the roofless concourse has few amenities, although the station does retain a staffed booking office, one toilet, soft drinks machine and a ticket issuing machine in the enclosed waiting area. (*MWC*)

A photograph, with much detail, taken before the overall roof at Lowestoft station was removed in 1992. A Class 101 diesel multiple unit can be seen in Platform Three and the resident diesel shunter, in this case a Class 08, is on the left. The 03 on the front of the Class 101 unit, indicates that the unit is formation 03. At that time, British Railways tried to maintain fixed sets of cars to make formations. (*PC*)

Platform One at Lowestoft Central, where Edward Thompson designed Class L1 2-6-4T No. 67714 is seen standing, is now part of the station car park as is the adjacent siding. Several of these powerful engines including No. 67714 were allocated to Lowestoft shed in the 1950s. They were used on all three routes out of Lowestoft and on summer Saturdays were occasionally used on the "Holiday Camps Express" on the coast line to Gorleston-on-Sea . (FC)

A busy Lowestoft Central in the 1950s with two Class N7 0-6-2T locomotives present and the sidings full of rolling stock. All track to the right of the signal box has been recovered and the land is now used as a car park. (FC)

Lowestoft was home to a number of Class N7 0-6-2T locomotives including N7/4 No. 69621, seen here on station pilot duties in Platform Three. This engine, the sole surviving member of the class, is preserved and in recent years has undergone a major overhaul in the Weybourne workshops of the North Norfolk Railway. The type was designed by A. J. Hill for the GER, however it was later subjected to a number of modifications and developments which resulted in the final class consisting of several variants. *(FC)*

For a great many years the footbridge which crosses the railway tracks as they approach Lowestoft Central station provided grand views of trains and locomotives. At the time of writing (2004) this fine facility, very much appreciated by those interested in railways, has been withdrawn and the bridge is now out of use. In the 1930s Great Eastern Holden designed Class F3 2-4-2T 8083, built in 1894 and withdrawn in 1938, leaves Lowestoft with a passenger train. *(MWC)*

A typical scene at Britain's most easterly station in the 1950s, as another of the Lowestoft allocated Class L1 2-6-4Ts, No. 67770, waits to leave with a Norwich train. (*DW*)

Another interesting scene from the "Iron Bridge", the once popular vantage point at Lowestoft. The coaching stock in the arriving train on the left, gives an indication of the type in service locally during the early 1950s. You can almost feel the footbridge shaking as Class K3 2-6-0 No. 61973 makes a spirited departure from Lowestoft Central and approaches the bridge. This locomotive was allocated to Lowestoft for many years and in late 1958 was transferred away. (*GM*)

On 10th August 1912, the 1.15pm troop train leaves Lowestoft for Norwich behind GER Class N31 (LNER Class J14) 0-6-0 No. 994. Built in 1894, No. 994 was scrapped in 1916. The train is about to pass the engine sheds, having just passed Coke Ovens Junction Signal Box which is seen on the left. (*LCGB/KN*)

Lowestoft sheds on 10th August 1912 with Class N31 0-6-0 No. 965, and GER Class 209 0-4-0ST No. 210 standing outside. The Class 209 was used on the harbour lines, some of which included tight curves.

No. 965 was built in 1896 and scrapped in 1921, No. 210 was built in 1875 by Neilson & Co. and scrapped in 1914. Under the LNER, the remaining locomotives of this this type became the Class Y5.

The turntable seen on the left was later repositioned further west. (*LCGB/KN*)

From 1908, this scene shows GER small boilered Class T19 2-4-0 No. 1038 and GER "Humpty Dumpty" large boiler Class T19 No. 778 outside Lowestoft sheds. Built in 1897, No. 1038 was scrapped in 1909 in the original condition it was built. No. 778 was built in 1892, and after being rebuilt around 1903 with large boiler, new firebox and cab, was scrapped in 1920. (*LCGB/KN*)

A similar scene, but many years later and with much more powerful locomotives. Britannia 7MT 4-6-2 No. 70035 *Rudyard Kipling* is seen together with Class B17/6 4-6-0 No. 61659 *East Anglian* outside the shed. No. 61659 was named *Norwich City* in 1936 when new, changing to *East Anglian* in 1937, at the same time as the locomotive was streamlined. The streamlining was removed in 1951, and *East Anglian* was withdrawn from traffic at Lowestoft in 1960 and scrapped at Stratford the same year. The site previously occupied by the sheds, turntable and yard is now a road. (*GM*)

Designed by Mr. R. A. Riddles during wartime for the Ministry of Supply, the Class WD 2-8-0 heavy freight locomotives were introduced during 1943. After the war many passed to the LNER and to British Railways in 1948. A rather dirty March based No. 90001 is seen visiting Lowestoft in the early 1950s. Over 700 of these powerful locomotives entered service with British Railways, and twenty five of a larger version with a 2-10-0 wheel arrangement. (*GM*)

A Class J19 0-6-0 arrives at Lowestoft off the Great Yarmouth line with empty coaching stock. It is not possible to tell if this had originated at Yarmouth, as it was common practice in the summer months for stock to be kept in sidings at Hopton and Gorleston when not required. (*BL*)

Class B17/6 4-6-0 No. 61620 *Clumber* about to reverse off Lowestoft turntable on 16th July 1956 after being turned. Entering service as Class B17/1 No. 2820 in November 1930, *Clumber* became No. 1620 in June 1946 and with nationalisation was renumbered No. 61620. After being reboilered in 1951, No. 61620 was reclassified as a B17/6. Withdrawal from service whilst at Kings Lynn came in November 1959 and breaking up for scrap took place at Stratford in February 1960. No examples of this well known class were retained for preservation. *(DW)*

Lowestoft shed (32C) was home to a number of different Class L1 2-6-4T locomotives over the years. On this occasion we find a visiting member of the class No. 67709, from Ipswich, on shed. Class L1s were used on a variety of tasks on the three lines which terminated at the town's station. (GM)

Gresley designed Class K3 2-6-0 No. 61926 arrives at Lowestoft with a goods train, having just passed the engine sheds. During 1955, five of these useful locomotives were allocated to Lowestoft with this engine being one of them. (GM)

Photographing locomotives at Lowestoft which were standing on the north side of the shed was not easy. From the south side, there was much shade, and on the north side across the main lines into the town the subject was in total shade. However, Class F6 2-4-2T No. 67231, one of the last two Holden designed tank locomotives to be based at Lowestoft, was recorded in that difficult position in 1957. (DW)

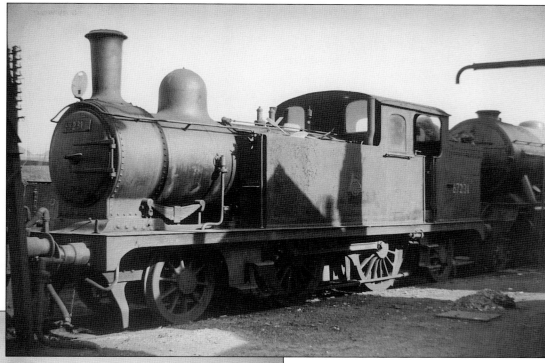

Class J17 0-6-0 No. 65559 leaves Lowestoft with a local goods train. This locomotive and two other Class J17s, Nos. 65507 and 65558, spent many years allocated to Lowestoft. (DW)

In May 1956 H. R. H. The Duke of Edinburgh undertook a number of royal visits including Lowestoft, where he opened the new South Pier Pavilion. Class B1 4-6-0 No. 61399, of Stratford shed, was used to haul the Royal Train from Wickham Market Junction to Lowestoft. The train had been stabled overnight on the Framlingham Branch. No. 61399 is seen here on shed at Lowestoft, in the company of Shedmaster Mr. Leverick on the left, Driver Charlie Jackson in the centre and Fireman Alfred Hubbard on the right. (*AHC*)

With the end of steam in sight, the sidings around Lowestoft shed became resting places for engines facing an uncertain fate. Class F6 2-4-2T No. 67234 leads a line of other S. D. Holden designed tank locomotives awaiting their fate. No. 67234 retains a Yarmouth Beach shed plate, the home for many years for this engine. (*NF*)

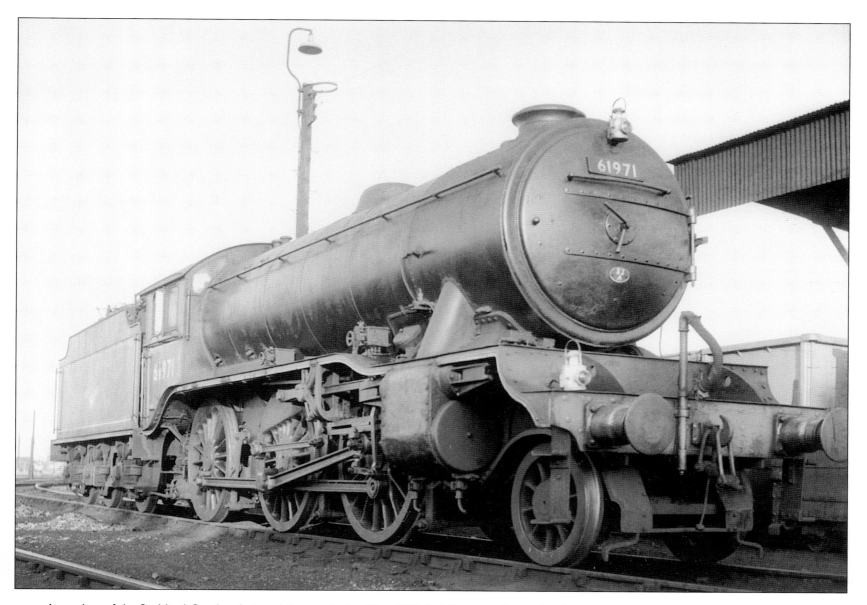

A number of the Sir Nigel Gresley designed three cylinder Class K3/2 2-6-0s were allocated to Lowestoft (32C). This locomotive, No. 61971, was a well kept Norwich based example when recorded visiting 32C in the 1950s. Developed from a previous Great Northern design, this type was introduced by the Great Northern Railway in 1924 and could cope equally well on fast freight or heavy passenger work. Regretfully no examples of these well liked machines were saved from the cutters torch. (*GM*)

Gresley's Class V2 2-6-2s, and his impressive Class K3 2-6-0s had the reputation that they could pull anything.

Introduced in the early 1920s, the K3 was a development of an earlier Great Northern design and was considered advanced for the time. In addition to the large boiler and 3 cylinders, the 5' 8" driving wheels gave them wide flexibility, although their RA8 rating could restrict their route availability. This view shows the driving wheels of Lowestoft's K3 No. 61959 with one of the regular crew of that engine, Mr. Alfred Hubbard. (AH)

Lowestoft's Class L1 2-6-4T No. 67707 hammers into Lowestoft from Beccles on 25th July 1959 with coaches off a London Liverpool Street to Yarmouth/Lowestoft service. These coaches were detached at Beccles from the main train. With the Beccles to Yarmouth South Town line closing in November, it would not be long before this practice would cease. The Lowestoft Sleeper Depot is on the left of the photograph and the allotments in the background, which were at one time railway property, have in recent years been built on. (MW)

Class K1 2-6-0 No. 62013 leaves Lowestoft with a Yarmouth South Town to London Liverpool Street service on 25th July 1959. Introduced in 1949, the Class K1 was a powerful mixed traffic engine with a 5P6F rating. Often referred to as a baby Class B1 locomotive the K1 was in fact more powerful than the B1. With 5'2" driving wheels it was sure footed and the 70 examples built were to be found in eastern England, the north east and Scotland, hauling anything from heavy coal trains from the pits to express passenger.
One of these well liked engines, No. 62005, is preserved. (MW)

The last British Railways steam locomotives seen at Lowestoft were Class B1 4-6-0s used as coaching stock heating units one of which, No. 61138, was resting in the sidings during the afternoon of 7th February 1965. Lowestoft engine shed officially closed in September 1960, but the facilities continued to be used by visiting locomotives well into 1962. The last steam hauled passenger train left the town in June 1962 hauled by a Class B1 4-6-0. (MW)

By 1984, with the progressive withdrawal of through services to the midlands, the north and London, Lowestoft had one long distance hauled through service remaining. That one service, to London Liverpool Street, is seen here waiting to depart with Class 31/1 AIA-AIA No. 31133. The Class 31 diesel electric locomotives were built during 1957-62 by Brush Traction. Powered by an English Electric 12SVT1470hp engine and fitted with a steam heating boiler, No. 31133 was providing steam heat to the coaching stock. This train was often hauled by a Class 37 locomotive, or sometimes a Class 47. On 12th May 1984, the last hauled through train ran. However in 1999, Anglia Railways announced that the service would be reinstated using the latest Class 170 DMUs. (*RF*)

Norwich DMU formation No. 30 comprising Cravens Class 105 DMBS 54122 and DTS 53359 leaves Lowestoft on 26th September 1987. This unit was unique at that time and had been completely refurbished and given the much admired brunswick green livery. The Class 105 was introduced in 1956. (*RP*)

Lowestoft remains the destination for specialised freight trains carrying material used in the offshore industries. Over the years a wide variety of types of diesel locomotives have been seen on these trains including Classes 31,37, 47, 58, 66 and 67. Main Line liveried Class 58 Co-Co No. 58001 is seen at Lowestoft on 25th March 1999 having just arrived on one of these workings. (NF)

Earlier diesel hauled Lowestoft freight and goods trains were sometimes hauled by Class 37 Co-Co locomotives one of which, No. 37059, is seen here waiting to depart adjacent to Lowestoft signal box on 11th November 1987.
This lengthy train consists of wagons for the carriage of grain and coal, and vans for Cantley sugar factory. Cantley no longer has rail access and coal together with vast quantities of grain are now conveyed by road to Lowestoft. (NF)

Fish was at one time transported by rail in great quantities from Lowestoft and Great Yarmouth. This scene from the 1950s, shows a Class J39 0-6-0 locomotive with fish being loaded into a van in the sidings at Lowestoft. Although some of the sidings are still in use today, the fish trains are now history, as is the once great fishing industry in both towns. (*BL*)

The General Motors built Class 66/0 Co-Co locomotives have taken over from British built traction such as Classes 31, 37 and 47 on the freight workings from Lowestoft. Motherwell allocated class member No. 66103, operated by English Welsh & Scottish Railways, leaves the town on 27th August 2003 with a typical working to Scotland. (*MW*)

The Coast Line

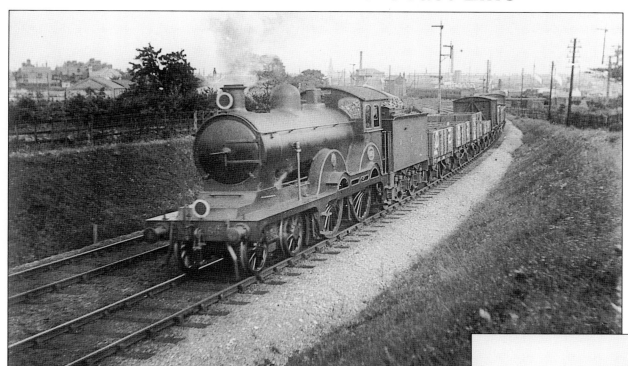

Above-GER Class S46 4-4-0 No. 1863 climbs away from Coke Ovens Junction at Lowestoft with a midday goods train for Yarmouth. In the distance can be seen Coke Ovens Junction Signal Box, which was demolished in 1968. Built by the GER in 1903 for express passenger work, under the LNER the S46 became Class D14. (*LCGB/KN*)

Right-An English Electric Class 37 Co-Co diesel electric locomotive heads a London Liverpool Street -Yarmouth South Town train at almost the same spot as No. 1863 seen above. (*RP*)

Class N7/3 No. 69679 approaches Lowestoft North with a Lowestoft Central to Yarmouth South Town train. The train is in the cutting at the back of Worthing Road which, in 2004, was converted into a cycleway and footpath. Most of the original railway bridges remain and the cycleway/footpath passes under them. No. 69679 was allocated to Lowestoft for many years and left in July 1957 when it was transferred to Stratford. The replacement at Lowestoft was No. 69706, previously a Norwich engine. (DW)

Lowestoft North station and yard covered a large area which today is covered by housing.
In steam days, Class D16/3 4-4-0 No. 62546 *Claud Hamilton* leaves Lowestoft North for Lowestoft Central with a train from Yarmouth South Town.
One of the familiar features of most intermediate stations on this line, a camping coach, is on the right. (SLS)

Class J15 0-6-0 No 65469 leaves Lowestoft North with a stopping train from Yarmouth South Town in 1957. After closure of the railway, all the land seen here was purchased for residential development. The roads there have names associated with the railway, such as Beeching Drive. No. 65469 was transferred to Lowestoft in July 1957 staying only until September, when it was reallocated to Norwich. No. 65469 was withdrawn from March shed in August 1962. (DW)

A Saturday afternoon in the summer of 1957 and Lowestoft's Class J17 0-6-0 No. 65559 heads the down "HCE" between Lowestoft North and Corton. It was not unusual for lineside fires to be started by engines working this heavy train along the coast line, especially when the locomotive was a Class J15 0-6-0.

On the left, building is in progress on properties in Gunton Drive, a road which was completed before the closure of the line in 1970 and today runs parallel with the location of the trackbed. Together with the trackbed, all land seen here has now been built on. (DW)

Without the aid of modern earth moving, building and engineering equipment, the railway builders of yesteryear achieved amazing results especially in the making of viaducts, tunnels and large bridges. The construction of the majority of the direct Great Yarmouth-Lowestoft railway line by the GER for the Norfolk & Suffolk Joint Railways Committee was considered a straightforward task by Oliver, the contractor. However, it was an expensive line to construct due to the cost of buying land, some of which was in the neighbourhood of urban areas. At Gorleston, land was £500 per acre and at Hopton, Corton and Gunton the cost was £270 per acre. Construction of over twenty bridges for a reasonably short line of 9 miles 11 chains also proved costly. The really expensive part of the project was the M&GN link from Gorleston North Junction to Yarmouth Beach where the Breydon, Vauxhall and Bure viaducts were built. In total £159,758-12s-4d was spent on just over 2 miles of track. The GER obtained the Act of Parliament in 1897 but construction was slow to commence. When it did however, progress was rapid and here we see the building of Corton station (top) and Lowestoft North (Middle and Bottom) around 1901. The author has information that the contractors locomotive seen here at Lowestoft North was able, with the agreement of the GER, to work on their metals at the Central station and the sidings there. (AGC, PKC, MWC)

Lowestoft North in the diesel era, with a Derby Lightweight multiple unit forming a Lowestoft Central - Yarmouth South Town service. (*EDPpics*)

With many holiday camps in the village, the station at Hopton-on-Sea saw vast crowds passing through on summer Saturdays. As with the other stations along the coastal line, Hopton had a goods siding where coal and sugar beet were the main commodities handled. The station is seen here in June 1962, during the short period when the line was considered a main line with regular express trains passing through. (SJ)

The line between Lowestoft Central and Yarmouth South Town became a long siding from Lowestoft for the last few years before closure. The service was extremely cheap to run, with no level crossings of any importance, all stations unmanned and a diesel multiple unit providing a shuttle service between the two towns. Immediately after closure and before the demolition teams moved in, Hopton-on-Sea is seen as a somewhat rundown unmanned halt, only a shadow of the once busy station it was. Today the need for the line is perhaps greater than ever, with the vast increase in population at villages along the coast, especially at Hopton, and with the District Hospital in the vicinity. (MWC)

Gorleston-on-Sea station opened with the line on 13th July 1903, and was considered the major station between Lowestoft and Great Yarmouth. It was the only one to have a cab rank. Together with an extensive yard and shed, it covered a large area, part of which now forms a roundabout and access roads. In addition to the nearby holiday camp, the station served the many hotels and boarding houses in the area.

The former trackbed to Yarmouth is now occupied by a dual carriageway road. Two other stations existed at Gorleston, one being Gorleston Links Halt which was a basic concrete platform with no facilities, and the other was Gorleston North. (SJ)

Gorleston North was a large station in the style of others on the line and had a flourishing goods yard supplying coal to the fishing industry. After suffering war damage it closed in 1942, never to reopen. The signal box there remained opened into the 1950s, as did the coal yard. (StationsUK)

Great Yarmouth/Lowestoft-Norwich-Ipswich
Great Yarmouth/Lowestoft-Norwich-Ely-March-Peterborough

A nostalgic and interesting view of Norwich Thorpe on 15th June 1955 with Norwich's Class D16/3 4-4-0 No. 62619 leaving with a mixed train and many steam locomotives visible at various locations in the yard and shed. The new siding on the right, yet to be ballasted, leads to the new fuelling point installed for the planned changeover to diesel powered multiple units and locomotives. Allocated to Norwich for many years, No. 62619 was withdrawn from service there in September 1957. (*EDPpics*)

With increasing population in the local area, Oulton Broad North remains one of the busiest small intermediate stations in East Anglia. In recent times, the level crossing at the station has been held responsible for causing delays to the very high volume of road traffic passing over the crossing. This is despite the fact that on average the crossing is closed to road traffic for an average of only three minutes to allow the passage of each train.

In 1974 the footbridge was removed, the level crossing modernised and the gates replaced by lifting barriers operated from the adjacent signal box. This scene, recorded in July 1961, shows the station prior to the waiting rooms mid way along both platforms being demolished. The first station at this location, was named Mutford, and situated on the other side of the level crossing. (AFF)

Very much now a celebrity locomotive based at the North Norfolk Railway, this scene shows Class B12/3 4-6-0 No. 61572 as an everyday hard working Norwich engine. Heading the Lowestoft - York through train, No. 61572 storms away from Oulton Broad North. (BL)

The main building at Somerleyton station is now in use as a private residence. The station is seen here complete with canopy, oil lamps, toilets and signal box, none of which survive today. The wooden shelter on the up platform, has been replaced by a bus shelter type building. (*StationsUK*)

Much of the countryside that the railway lines to Great Yarmouth and Lowestoft pass through is at present unspoilt and undeveloped. An example is the area around Somerleyton, where a Lowestoft bound Class 101 Metro-Cammell DMU is seen crossing the swing bridge over the River Waveney. In contrast, the East Suffolk line in particular now passes close to areas of wide scale development in a number of locations. Rail operators consider this an advantage, since hopefully it will increase passenger numbers. (*PC*)

This scene at Haddiscoe shows English Electric Class 37/0 Co-Co No. 37138 in May 1987 whilst heading for Norwich with a railtour. Just visible above the middle section of the train are the bridge supports previously used to carry the Yarmouth - Beccle line across low ground and the river. At one time Haddiscoe had two stations, one of these was on the Yarmouth South Town - Beccles line and the other on the Lowestoft - Norwich line. Service was withdrawn from the station served by the Yarmouth - Beccles line when that line closed on 2nd November 1959.

No. 37138 was completed at Vulcan Foundry in May 1963 as D6838, and was scrapped in 1994. (NF)

Of the two routes between Great Yarmouth and Norwich, the line via Reedham and Berney Arms opened in 1844 and the more direct line via Acle in 1883. Both are single track. Acle station has retained much of the steam age atmosphere as is seen in this view showing Class 47/7 No. 47714 heading a special through the station on 13th July 2003. (MW)

Top-The somewhat isolated and remote station at Berney Arms is situated between Yarmouth Vauxhall and Reedham. It is 15 miles 12 chains from Norwch. (*SJ*)

Bottom- Lingwood station is on the more direct of the two lines to Great Yarmouth and 7 miles 78 chains from Norwich. It is situated between Acle and Brundall. (*MWC*)

Brundall station is the junction where the more direct line to Great Yarmouth leaves the double track line to Lowestoft. From the mid 1950s, this photograph shows the station with the siding on the right in use. The station building is today not in railway use and the two shelters in the centre of the photograph no longer exist. A rather well designed wooden structure is now situated on this platform. (*StationsUK*)

An overall scene of the coaling tower and one of the turntables at Norwich Thorpe (32A) shed in the late 1950s. Classes of locomotive visible from left to right are J17 0-6-0, B1 4-6-0 and a K3 2-6-0. The spire of Norwich Cathedral is on the far right. (*FC*)

Class K3 2-6-0 No. 61840 approaches the platforms at Norwich in the mid 1950s with a passenger train. Class L1 2-6-4 No. 67714 is near the signal box and just visible on the right the tender of a Class B12/3 4-6-0. On the left are recently introduced Derby Lightweight diesel multiple units. With the change to electric and diesel traction, and the sheds and yard now replaced by modern supermarkets, retail shopping centres, nightclubs, industrial units and restaurants, the atmosphere at Norwich has changed completely. (*FC*)

An unusual scene at Norwich Thorpe as Class L1 2-6-4T No. 67706 waits with Ivatt Class 4MT 2-6-0 No. 43160 to back out of Platform Four, having arrived double heading a train. The Ivatt was at that time allocated to Yarmouth Beach shed (32F) and the Class L1 to Ipswich. Just visible above the cab of the L1 is the spire of Norwich Cathedral. (*GM*)

At Norwich Thorpe station pilot Class J15 0-6-0 No. 65469 is seen removing stock from one of the platforms. Introduced in July 1883 by the GER as the Class Y14, this versatile type was still at work in eastern England well into the diesel era. No. 65469 was withdrawn from service at March in August 1962. (AG)

Parkeston Quay (30F) allocated Class B1 4-6-0 No. 61149 at Norwich in company with a Class J17 0-6-0. No. 61149 was a 30F engine for over 10 years. (AG)

One of a number of locomotives on loan to the Eastern Region from the Southern during the late 1940s and early 1950s, Battle of Britain Class 4-6-2 No. 34059 *Sir Archibald Sinclair* waits to depart from Norwich on 18th May 1949 with "The Norfolkman", a fast train to London only stopping at Ipswich. Complete with name boards, the York - Lowestoft through train is just leaving the adjacent platform for Lowestoft, headed by Class D16/3 4-4-0 No. 62581. (*LCGB/KN*)

The diesel traction era has arrived at Norwich as a new Brush Type 2 diesel electric locomotive is seen taking on fuel in the siding on the right. However, much steam activity remains around the station and the sheds. The station pilot, H. N. Gresley GNR designed Class J50/2 0-6-0 No. 68905 clears Gresley and BR Mark I coaching stock from one of the platforms. The Class J50/2 was introduced in 1922 and No. 68905 was one of the batch rebuilt from the smaller Class J51 which were built between 1915 and 1922. (*FC*)

A crowded Norwich Thorpe station in the years following the Second World War and shortly after the nationalisation of the railways, when the great majority of the population travelled by rail instead of the private motorcar. Unlike today, when some fares go uncollected, barrier checks are being carried out ensuring that all those on the platforms have tickets to travel or at least a platform ticket, available from the machine at 1d. each. Special springtime excursion fares are advertised to Great Yarmouth, Lowestoft, Mundesley, Cromer and Sheringham, with the return fare to Yarmouth Vauxhall being 3/-. In addition to the crowded concourse, there appears to be little room left for further passengers on platform five. The next train advertised to leave platform four is the "The East Anglian", an express with refreshment car facilities and stopping only at Ipswich on the journey to London Liverpool Street. The motive power would probably have been one of the new Thompson Class B1 4-6-0s or a Gresley Class B17 or B2 4-6-0. (EDPpics)

During the 1950s, Ipswich based Class B17/6 4-6-0 No. 61669 *Barnsley* was usually to be found at work hauling London Liverpool Street to Great Yarmouth and Lowestoft trains on the East Suffolk line. On this occasion, a rather dirty *Barnsley* is seen arriving at Norwich Thorpe with an express passenger train. No. 61669 started life in May 1937 as LNER No. 2869 and was renumbered 1669 in 1946. In 1949, *Barnsley* was rebuilt as a Class B17/6 and renumbered 61669. It was withdrawn from service at Ipswich in September 1958 and scrapped at Doncaster in November that year. (FC)

Two well known East Anglian diesel types, the Class 37 on the left, and Class 47 on the right, at the buffers at Norwich. Both types were commonly used on passenger and freight trains in East Anglia. However, with the general replacement of hauled rolling stock by multiple units, widespread electrification, and the introduction of new classes of diesel locomotives, their use declined. On occasion, Class 47 power can still be witnessed in Norfolk and Suffolk when operational needs cannot be met with the normally available traction and multiple units, and for special services. (RF)

Electrification of the Norwich to Ipswich line required the bridge at Trowse to be replaced. A Class 105 DMU crosses the bridge with the new one under construction alongside. The date is 23rd February 1986. (*NF*)

The signal box at Trowse was a long standing feature of the Norwich railway scene. It became redundant with the resignalling of the line, associated with the electrification scheme. The box, complete with a fine display of plants inside, is seen here on 23rd February 1986. (*NF*)

Situated between the stations of Tivetshall and Flordon on the Norwich to Ipswich section of the former Great Eastern main line, Forncett represents one of several stations that have closed on this line. Others between Norwich and Ipswich include Mellis (junction for Eye), Burston, Swainsthorpe, Finningham, Haughley, Claydon, Bramford, Tivetshall(junction for Beccles) and Flordon. Forncett was situated 104 miles from London Liverpool Street and was the junction for the GER 6¾ mile line to Wymondham, on the Norwich to Ely line. *(StationsUK)*

In recent years, and especially since the introduction of electric hauled services between London and Norwich, Diss has become popular with people who live in the area and commute to London by rail. It was at one time a junction for the 7 mile long private Scole Railway, which opened in 1850 and closed in 1886. British Railways blue liveried Class 37/0 Co-Co No. 37308 passes through the station at high speed on 9th April 2002 after participating in a railtour. *(MW)*

British Railways two tone green liveried Class 47/7 Co-Co No. D1102/47519 ambles through Stowmarket, on 15th June 1996 whilst participating in the EUR150 celebrations when steam hauled trains ran between Bury St. Edmunds and Ipswich hauled by Class 7MT 4-6-2 No. 70000 *Britannia* and a major exhibition of locomotives and rolling stock was held at Ipswich. Class 47 locomotives were seen regularly at locations such as this before electrification of the Norwich to Ipswich line. North of Stowmarket at Haughley, is situated the important junction for the lines to Ely and Cambridge. Haughley was also the junction for the charming Mid Suffolk Light Railway to Laxfield which closed to passengers in 1952. (MW)

Wymondham is one of the larger stations and also a junction on the Norwich - Ely line. This splendid scene from the early 1900s shows two handsome horse drawn carriages and a few of the station staff outside the main station building. The branch line to Wells-on-Sea, which closed to passengers in October 1964, left the main line at this point. Sections of this branch remain in use as the Mid Norfolk Railway and, at the extreme northern end, as the narrow gauge Wells and Walsingham Light Railway. (MWC)

Wymondham in the 21st century with Class 66/0 Co-Co No. 66126 rattling the station as it passes through with an aggregates train on 20th November 2001. These 3250hp diesel electric locomotives were built by General Motors in London, Ontario with a General Motors AR8/C86 engine and General Motors alternator and traction motors. (*MW*)

The line through Attleborough station opened in 1845 and since the closure in 1959 of the former M&GN, which served many parts of Norfolk, the line has been the only direct rail route into the County from the midlands and the north. Being served by trains running between the cities of Norwich and Cambridge and cross country services between East Anglia, the midlands and the north west, Attleborough is well served by rail. In this view, an Anglia Railways Derby built Class 170/2 three car diesel multiple unit working a service between Cambridge and Norwich, waits while many passengers board. (*MW*)

Britannia Class 7MT No. 70037 *Hereward the Wake* approaches Thetford with a London Liverpool Street - Norwich via Cambridge service. From the autumn of 1958, the great majority of through services between London and Norwich over this route ceased. More economical use of locomotives and rolling stock was achieved by running the direct Liverpool Street to Norwich trains via Ipswich. However, Norwich to London via Cambridge remains a useful diversionary feature of the East Anglian rail map and was used as such in 2004. At one time, Thetford was a junction station with lines to Bury St. Edmunds and Swaffham. The line to Bury closed to passengers in 1953 and that to Swaffham in 1964. (*MWC*)

Ely remains a very important East Anglian junction for both passenger and heavy freight traffic. In steam days, Norwich based Britannia Class 7MT No. 70009 *Alfred The Great* is seen heading for home north of Ely with a London Liverpool Street - Norwich via Cambridge express on a murky day in August 1961. The Ely avoiding line, at that time double track, can be seen on the right. Ely is 70 miles 30 chains from London Liverpool Street. (*MWC*)

GB Railfreight operated Class 66/7 Co-Co No. 66710 heads a train from the midlands for the east coast through Ely on 28th February 2004. Sights such as this are common at Ely, with the livery of the freight locomotives of the different operators providing colourful contrasts. (MW)

Ely station on 4th July 1976 showing the middle line through the station, semaphore signals, the resident Class 08 0-6-0 shunter and a Class 37 hauled passenger train. With electrification of the line through Ely, much of this scene changed. (RP)

March was at one time an important junction, but today many of the cross country services no longer stop there. From the convenient footbridge at the station, Class D16/3 4-4-0 No. 62597 is seen leaving March with a train for Ely. For many years this locomotive was allocated to Yarmouth South Town. (MWC)

When use of the East Coast Main Line has been restricted, trains have been diverted through March. On 24th July 1977, Class 55 Co-Co No. 55007 Pinza passes through whilst heading a train for London Kings Cross. These locomotives were built in 1961-62 and are powered by two 18cyl Napier "Deltic" engines producing a total of 3,300hp. Six of the production locomotives are in preservation, but Pinza was broken up.(RP)

Steam and diesel locomotives allocated to March frequently worked goods and passenger trains to Lowestoft and Yarmouth. The number of diesel and steam locomotives allocated to March was considerable. The shed (31B) closed to steam in November 1963, but a large number of diesel locomotive could still be found there. In 1966, included in the allocation at March were twenty four Class 31s and ten Class 37s. This view of the depot, then known by the code MR, shows seven Class 37s, three Class 31s and one 08. The date is 24th July 1977. (*RP*)

Peterborough has for long been considered the main railway gateway to the Eastern Counties. At Peterborough North station on 20th May 1938, we find M&GN Class DA No. 083. The "0" was added to the number in 1936. This engine was ordered for the GNR as their Class J4, but became one of twelve diverted to the M&GN where they became Class DA. No. 083, seen here fitted with a flowerpot chimney, was built by Dubs in 1901. In 1907 it was fitted with an extended smokebox and during 1921 was reboilered. Under British Railways, No. 083 became Class J3 No. 64158 and was scrapped in 1951. (*MWC*)

This scene captures the atmosphere at Peterborough in the days when Gresley Class A4 4-6-2 locomotives were seen daily at the Station. Before the days of electric signalling, Class A4 No. 60033 *Seagull* of King Cross shed stands in the station having just arrived with a train for the north. The experimental diesel electric locomotive *Deltic* was built in 1955 by English Electric and today is part of the National Collection at York. It weighs 107 tonnes and had a rated maximum speed of 105mph. *Deltic* became the prototype of twenty-two production locomotives, and is seen here complete with oil lamps, passing through Peterborough with an up express during the trials period. (*GM*)

To travel between Lowestoft or Great Yarmouth and the north, a change of trains is often necessary at Peterborough. Before the electrification of the East Coast Main Line, the mainstay of services on this route was provided by the Inter-City 125 units (High Speed Trains). Introduced in 1977, these units can comprise of seven, eight or nine Mk. 111 coaches with a power car at each end. Each power car contains the Paxman Valenta 12cyl. 12RP200LM 2250bhp diesel engine. One of these highly successful units, still looking futuristic in the 21st century, approaches Peterborough from Scotland or the north of England forming a London Kings Cross service. (PC)

We leave Peterborough with another image reflecting the atmosphere of the steam age showing the North Box, and one of the small number of Gresley Class V2 2-6-2 locomotives fitted with a double chimney. (GM)

Colour Interlude

The Britannia Class 7MT 4-6-2 locomotives became a common sight on main line services between Yarmouth South Town/Lowestoft and Liverpool Street as increasing numbers of diesel locomotives took over their traditional work on the former GER Norwich main line. In May 1959, not many months before the withdrawal of passenger services and closure of this section of line, No. 70011 *Hotspur* heads a Yarmouth South Town-London Liverpool Street express through the superb setting of St. Olaves cutting. (*EA/CR*)

A location that today is part of a vast housing estate. Hopton station in October 1956, in the days when it was the centre of a small quiet village. In the summer months, Hopton was very popular with the thousands of holidaymakers who stayed at the many holiday camps in the village, including the large camp adjacent to the station. The majority of these campers would arrive at Hopton station on through trains from such places as Birmingham, Derby, Leicester and London. H. A. Ivatt GNR design C12 4-4-2T No. 67366, a type introduced in 1898, leaves for Lowestoft with a push pull set on this bright autumn day. (EA/CR)

On the last day of services over the former M&GN in February 1959, and for the remaining few final hours, Class N7/3 0-6-2T No. 69698 is employed on providing the shuttle service between South Lynn and Kings Lynn stations. Within days No. 69698 was reallocated to Hatfield, where it stayed until December 1960. It was then moved to Kings Cross, staying until March 1961. The final move was to Stratford, where No. 69698 was withdrawn from service during September 1961. (RR/CR)

Superb sea views were obtained whilst travelling north from Yarmouth on the former M&GN main line where it runs close to the beach and cliffs. Working a Yarmouth Beach - Leicester summer Saturday's only train, Ivatt 4MT 2-6-0 No. 43154 makes a splendid subject on the cliffs at California in glorious sunshine on this Saturday in August 1958. Unfortunately, 1958 turned out to be the last summer that such services would run and scenes like this could be witnessed. *(EA/CR)*

London Liverpool Street is rarely portrayed during the 1930s in colour. However, this rare image shows LNER green liveried Class B12/3 4-6-0 No. 8518 and black D16/3 4-4-0 No. 8871 in the station. An interesting selection of coaching stock is in the adjacent two platforms.(*EB/CR*)

The London Liverpool Street to Gorleston "Holiday Camps Express" or as it was known locally "HCE", rolls into Hopton on a glorious summer day in July 1957. Today every aspect of this scene including the embankments has been erased from the village by residential development. Houses now occupy the fields, woods and the former railway land. Motive power from Lowestoft is provided by Class J17 0-6-0 No. 65558, a well known local engine, that was withdrawn from service in January 1960. It was normal for local children with home made carts to meet these trains and carry holidaymaker's luggage to the camps for a few pence. (*EA/CR*)

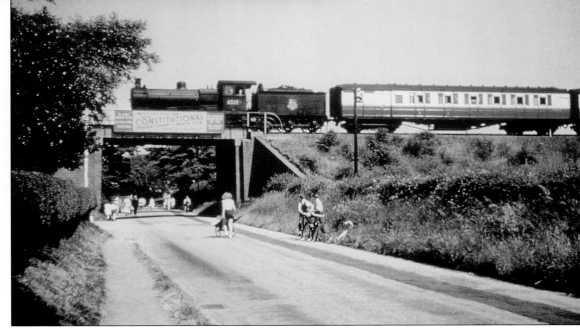

A delightful scene from 1955 at Stratford as Class B12/3 No. 61571, of Ipswich shed, heads out of London with a down express surrounded by Gresley coaching stock. No. 61571 was withdrawn from service at Norwich in November 1959, at a time when the remaining members of the class were being withdrawn from service. After spending December 1959 in store at Stratford it was scrapped there the following month. It became one of the last two of the class to be scrapped leaving the now celebrity B12/3, No. 61572, to live on in preservation. *(BrC/CR)*

The "HCE" was normally routed from Gorleston to Lowestoft and then took the direct route via the East Suffolk Line to London Liverpool Street. Unlike today, if for any reason this path was not available, alternatives could easily be found. With a fine exhibition of power and speed, Lowestoft's Class K3 2-6-0 No. 61973 roars through the pleasantly situated Harlow station with the diverted "HCE" from Gorleston-on-sea, Hopton, Corton, and Lowestoft in brilliant sunshine on a Saturday in July 1957. A good example of a flexible, serving railway intent on maintaining a customer friendly service without using buses and coaches. *(PGL/CR)*

Just after crossing St. Olaves swing bridge, Class B17/6 4-6-0 No. 61665 *Leicester City,* makes for Yarmouth South Town with a down express in June 1957. The superb condition of *Leicester City*, a South Town engine, is noteworthy. It was not normal to see a locomotive polished to this extent whilst in every day use. Locally, Lowestoft's Class K3 2-6-0 No. 61959 was considered for many years the cleanest and most polished engine. *(EA/CR)*

A rare colour photograph of Class 40 1Co-Co1 No. D202 in July 1958 working a Norwich-London Liverpool Street service on Belstead Bank. This was the first year in which these locomotives were available for use on the former Great Eastern main line, and for a number of years they were to work side by side with Britannia Class 7MT 4-6-2 steam locomotives. These Type 4 diesel electric locomotives weighed 132 tons and are 69 ft. 6 inches long. Seven examples of this English Electric design are in preservation. D202 later became No. 40002. (MWC)

Stratford's celebrity Class 47/4 Co-Co No, 47581 *Great Eastern,* at Ipswich on 8th March 1986 whilst in charge of a Norwich-London Liverpool Street service. This locomotive was allocated to the Network, Great Eastern sector at that time. (*NF*)

A scene that can never be repeated since Lowestoft station no longer has a roof! Norwich Class 101 Metro Cammell DMU formations Nos. 84 (51209 and 54083), and 89(51229 and 54055), at the buffer stops on 21st April 1985. (*NF*)

Although not in this livery, Class 47 Co-Co diesel locomotives are still a familiar sight at Yarmouth when used to haul specials and London through trains to and from Norwich. Class 47/4 No 47576 *Kings Lynn* was at Yarmouth in Network South East livery on 25th May 1987. (*NF*)

A one time common sight throughout much of East Anglia, the Class 25 diesel electric locomotives had a considerable following amongst local railway enthusiasts. Often stabled overnight at March, they were a familiar sight at Norwich and Yarmouth on summer Saturdays when responsible for haulage of many of the cross-country services. Class members Nos. 25184 and 25235 are seen at Norwich, set amongst many reminders of a past railway era, after arriving from the midlands with a passenger train for Yarmouth. (*RF*)

Another bygone railway scene at Norwich with Stratford's Class 37/0 Co-Co No. 37219 arriving with a mixed goods on 9th August 1985. (*NF*)

Built during 1958-62 for main line passenger use, the Class 40 1Co-Co1 locomotives were powered by an English Electric 16cyl 16SVT Mk.2 2000hp diesel engine driving six EE 526/5D traction motors. Originally identified as Type 4s and numbered D200-399, this class was responsible for the demise of main line steam traction in many locations. They were allocated to several regions, including Scotland, with the initial batch, D200-209 being allocated to the Eastern Region. Building of the Class 40s was shared between Robert Stephenson & Hawthorn and Vulcan Foundry. They had steam heating boilers and a maximum speed of 90mph. No. 40006 was recorded at Lowestoft in October 1979. (RP)

Distribution of newspapers was once an important task for the railways and newspaper vans were just part of the railway scene. With the loss of this business, the vans became part of British railway history. At Lowestoft on 14th August 1982, having been used for delivering the newspapers to the town in the early morning, the van is seen waiting to be returned for use in the next deliveries. Class 37 Co-Co No. 37041 passes, possibly running round to collect the van. (RP)

At one time many Class 37s were assigned for the haulage of container traffic. However they have now been generally superseded by imported diesel locomotives. Recalling a once familiar scene at Ipswich is class member No. 37031, waiting on the centre road to enter the tunnel. Originally designated Type 3, the Class 37s were a common sight on goods and passenger work in East Anglia. At the time of writing, many remain in service with different operators, and several are now in preservation. (RF)

Powered by a Gardner 8L3 204hp diesel engine and using mechanical transmission, the 30ton Class 03 shunter was a common sight in yards and sidings in many regions. Stabled near Lowestoft station in October 1982, class member No. 03370 keeps company with the stock of the early morning Lowestoft -London Liverpool Street through train. These locomotives were introduced in 1957. (AG)

A nostalgic view of Norwich on 19th September 1985 during the period when traction was totally provided by diesel power and before the paraphernalia of electrification arrived. Locomotives seen are Class 03 0-6-0 No. 03399, Class 31/4 A1A-A1A No. 31415, Class 47/4 Co-Co No. 47610 and an unidentified Class 37. A Class 101 Metro Cammell DMU is in the foreground and the yard is full of a wide variety of goods and freight wagons, which includes coal hoppers and oil tankers.(*NF*)

Although this scene portrays a modern electrified railway, the rolling stock and livery is now dated. A British Railways standard design Class 312/1 Outer Suburban Four-Car Unit No. 312791 is seen at Ipswich waiting to form a return service to London Liverpool Street in July 1985. In many ways these "slam door" units, which were introduced in 1975, were more comfortable than the units that replaced them. (*RP*).

A superb scene to delight the many Class 37 diesel electric fans, as No. 37114 *City of Worcester* draws to a halt at Halesworth, on arrival from Lowestoft on 15th January 2004. This 1750hp English Electric Co-Co locomotive was involved in crew training duties. The Class 37s have a long association with the East Suffolk line. (*MW*)

A winter 1986 view of Lowestoft with a Class 105 Cravens DMU leaving for Norwich. (*RP*)

The English Electric/BR Class 86/2 electric locomotives were for many years a common sight on the Norwich to London Liverpool Street intercity route. In the early 21st century their replacement came in the form of GEC /BREL Class 90/0 electric locomotives, although some services on this route were already worked by Adtranz Class 170/2 DMUs. Anglia Railways No. 86230 arrives at Ipswich from Norwich with a London Liverpool Street train on 8th March 2004, in the last few months of the type's long association with the route. (MW)

In 2004, the majority of the local services to Great Yarmouth and Lowestoft were provided by British Rail Engineering Class 150 DMUs and the Leyland single car Class 153s. The 153s were originally the individual cars of the Class 155 two-car units. A trio of Class 153 units, with 153311 leading, are seen arriving at Acle on 13th July 2003. The individual liveries of the units are almost as colourful as the delightful display of flowers on the platform. (MW)

Great Yarmouth/Lowestoft-Beccles-Ipswich-London Liverpool Street

One of Lowestoft's Class K3 2-6-0s, No. 61959, on the East Suffolk line with a fish train on 24th May 1952.
A number of these powerful three cylinder locomotives were allocated to Lowestoft (*AHC*)

The first level crossing between Lowestoft and Beccles is Gravel Pit crossing at Oulton Broad seen here in the early 1960s. It is 116 miles 12 chains from Liverpool Street. (SJ)

A view looking towards Gravel Pit crossing and in the distance, Oulton Broad Swing Bridge signal box. A down Derby Lightweight diesel multiple unit, possibly working a through Yarmouth South Town service from Ipswich is approaching Oulton Broad North junction, which is 116 miles 27 chains from London Liverpool Street. The Lowestoft - Norwich line is joined for the approach to Lowestoft Central. (SJ)

Two views from a moving steam hauled London Liverpool Street to Yarmouth South Town train on the approaches to Lowestoft.
Top-Oulton Broad Swing Bridge
Bottom-Oulton Broad North Junction. (*PB*)

Barnby Signal Box was between Oulton Broad and Beccles and is seen here before the East Suffolk line was "rationalised" to a basic railway with long sections of single track, and radio token signalling replacing the manually operated signal boxes. (*SJ*)

The former signal box at Oulton Broad Swing Bridge remains today although no longer controlling any signals. However, this scene was recorded before the introduction of radio signalling on the East Suffolk line, when the box was still in use. This double track bridge was built in 1903 and replaced an earlier one which was single track, as indeed the present one now is.(*SJ*)

Stratford's Class 47/4 Co-Co No. 47579 *James Nightall G. C.* crosses Oulton Broad Swing Bridge with an up train for London Liverpool Street. The hulk in the foreground is the remains of a fishing vessel, possibly a steam drifter. (*PC*)

Originally named Carlton Colville, Oulton Broad South station is today a Token Exchange Point on the Radio Electronic Token Block system now used for train control on the East Suffolk line. The view shows the station before the line was fully modernised and the section between this station and Halesworth reduced to single track. *(PC)*

Oulton Broad South station on 7th January 2004 with English Electric Class 37 Co-Co locomotive No. 37684 *Peak National Park* arriving to stop and obtain the single line token for the long section to Halesworth. The buildings on the down platform are in use as a hairdressers, and those on the up platform for residential use. *(MW)*

Services were withdrawn from the Yarmouth Southown - Beccles line in November 1959 and amongst the stations closed was St. Olaves. Overnight, Great Yarmouth lost a direct important main line link with the capital, and stations such as St. Olaves, which had just become accustomed to diesel hauled trains after years of steam hauled expresses, goods, van and local trains, soon presented a sorry state. With the track on the other side of the level crossing to Belton and Burgh, and Yarmouth Southtown recovered, the station soon developed an air of being unwanted. The well known named express "The Easterling", would no longer thunder through the station, which was 115¼ miles from London Liverpool Street. After demolition of the building and platforms, the land was used for residential development. The only trace of the railway here now is a station nameboard displayed at the nearby garage. (*EDPpics*)

A much earlier view of St. Olaves, this time from the level crossing at the north end of the station. It is unlikely that closure of the station and the main line would have been taken at all seriously, at the time this scene was recorded around 1900. (*LESMS*)

The view from a London Liverpool Street bound train near Aldeby, on on 1st November 1959, the last day of services over the Yarmouth South Town - Beccles Line (*DW*)

Aldeby station closed to passengers along with other intermediate stations on the line between Yarmouth South Town and Beccles on 1st November 1959. It is seen here from one of the last through passenger trains to London to pass over the line. Aldeby station, 9¼ miles from South Town, remained in use for intermittent goods traffic until February 1965. (DW)

Beccles station on a dismal overcast day in February 1967, showing the Waveney Valley line disappearing behind the signal box, and the line to Lowestoft going off to the right The island platform waiting room was demolished many years ago and the platform is now derelict and overgrown.
The bay platform is in the bottom left of the photograph with the line going to the maltings in the bottom left corner. The other siding at one time served the cattle dock. The bay is now filled in. (MW)

The station staff took great pride in the floral displays, the appearance of the flowerbeds and Beccles station generally. This delightful image of the early 1950s is completed by the sight of the Waveney Valley line in the centre, curving away behind Beccles North Signal Box. (MWC)

Beccles station with T. W. Worsdell designed Class J15 0-6-0 No. 65460 in the sidings with a pick up goods on 16th February 1957. It was unfortunate that Beccles station, once an important junction, was nominated during 2003 in a local television competition as the worst eyesore in the town. The unmanned station, now consisting of a single platform, has in recent times suffered from persistent vandalism.
No. 65460 started life in 1912 as GER No. 562 and in 1924 became LNER No. 7562. It spent a number of years allocated to Lowestoft, leaving there in September 1960. (DW)

With several Class B12/3 4-6-0 locomotives shedded at Ipswich it was normal to see them in daily use on the East Suffolk line. Indeed as late as 1957, Ipswich still had ten of these popular machines. The filthy condition of No. 61561 waiting to leave Beccles for Yarmouth South Town indicates that by the 1956, cleaning of locomotives at Ipswich was not taken too seriously. By 1959 the facilities seen here on the left for providing water to engines had been demolished. In the distance, a Class J15 0-6-0 can be seen outside the shed. (DW)

The Lowestoft coaches of "The Easterling", a fast through train to Lowestoft and Great Yarmouth from London Liverpool Street, leave Beccles behind Class F3 2-4-2T No. 67127 on 13th September 1952. This train was scheduled to run non stop between London Liverpool Street and Beccles where it divided, one part going to Yarmouth South Town and the other, as seen here to Lowestoft. (PKC)

Right - With a light covering of snow on the ground, Class 150/2 Sprinter No 150257, *Queen Boadicea* arrives at Beccles on 25th January 2004. Powered by Cummins NT855R5 285hp engines and built by BREL York, these 75mph units form the backbone of local services throughout the old Anglia part of the "One" railway. (MW)

Bottom Left - A reminder of the once busy goods office, a wagon turntable at the now demolished maltings. (GM)

Bottom Right - Part of Beccles station in 2004, showing a housing development on the site of maltings and a Class 37 locomotive passing through. A similar scene showing the maltings is featured elsewhere in this book. (MW)

Britannia Class 7MT 4-6-2 locomotives became quite a common sight on the East Suffolk line in the last few years of the London through services to Great Yarmouth and Lowestoft. No. 70036 *Boadicea* is seen collecting the carriages from Lowestoft for attaching to the Yarmouth part of the London bound train. (*BL*)

Heavy freight on the East Suffolk line, as a train carrying steel ingots hauled by a Class 37/0 Co-Co diesel electric locomotive passes through the station at Brampton. This scene shows the line before the rationalisation of the early 1980s, which resulted in this section of line being singled and the removal of the down platform, from which this photograph was taken. The steel had been imported through the docks at Lowestoft. (*AHC*)

GER rebuilt Class T19 4-4-0 No. 766 arrives at Halesworth on 14th July 1911, with the 1110am Yarmouth South Town to Ipswich train. Under the LNER, this type of engine became the Class D13. Once an important location with a large rail served dairy next to the station, and the terminus of the narrow gauge Southwold Railway, Halesworth is now a Token Exchange Point on the Radio Token Signalling system used on the East Suffolk line, and one end of a long single line section of track to Lowestoft. The site of the dairy is now a housing estate and the railway to Southwold, which opened on 24th September 1879, closed on 11th April 1929. *(LCGB/KN)*

Saxmundham station has seen a number of important changes since the modernisation/rationalisation of the East Suffolk line. The former signal box is now the control and communications centre for train control on the line between Oulton Broad South and Westerfield and the branch to Sizewell. The platforms are now opposite each other with the present down platform replacing the earlier staggered and now demolished one. Direct Rail Services refurbished Class 20/3 Bo-Bo Nos. 20304 and 20309 are in the up platform having just come off the branch from Sizewell. This now freight only branch recreates the once common sight of a light or minor railway wandering through the countryside. *(MW)*

A classic East Suffolk line scene south of Woodbridge, showing Class D16/3 4-4-0 No. 62521 with a mixed train in the pre-nationalisation era as LNER No. 2521. The Class D16/3 were a Gresley rebuild of the Class D15, which themselves were a development of the original James Holden GER "Claud Hamilton" Class. *(JH/EMJ)*

Gresley Class K3 2-6-0 No. 61958 is seen on the East Suffolk line near Woodbridge with a fish train on 5th May 1951. This locomotive was allocated to Lowestoft for over 10 years and finally transferred away in February 1960 when the need for these locomotives was in decline due to the rundown of steam traction, and the continued loss to road transport of the carriage of goods such as fish. *(AHC)*

The Class L1 2-6-4T locomotives were a common type in Suffolk with many shedded locally. This scene from the early 1950s shows class member No. 67726 at Woodbridge with an Ipswich to Yarmouth South Town stopping train. Much of the original station remains at Woodbridge, which is 78 miles 78 chains from London Liverpool Street. Double track remains to Ipswich, but the section north to Saxmundham has been singled. *(JH/EMJ)*

A down express headed by Britannia 7MT 4-6-2 No. 70005 *John Milton* leaves Woodbridge with a train from Liverpool Street to Lowestoft and Great Yarmouth. *(JH/EMJ)*

A superb 1957 scene showing Stratford's Class B1 4-6-0 No. 61236 arriving at Colchester on an up express. On the far right, the posters showing the two available Holiday Runabout Ticket areas at £22/6d each, provide nostalgic reminders of rail travel opportunities to such destinations as Wells, California Halt, Hunstanton, Fakenham, Aldeburgh and Felixstowe Beach. (JWS/Foxline)

Since it is not generally visible to rail passengers passing through Ipswich, many would not be aware of the existence of the Lower Goods Yard. Diesel mechanical 0-6-0 shunter No. 11141, built by the Hunslet Engine Co. Ltd. with a Gardner 8L3 204hp engine, is seen at work in the well filled yard. A number of these shunters, which later became the Class 05, are now preserved. (FC)

The vast improvement made to the London to Norwich services, with the introduction in 1951 of the Britannia Class 7MT 4-6-2 locomotives, is well documented. One of regular engines on this link was No. 70011 *Hotspur,* seen here in the late 1950s about to enter Ipswich Tunnel. After many years based at Norwich she, like many in the class, finished her days on the Midland Region. *(MWC)*

Prior to electrification, the Class 47/4 Co-Co diesel electric locomotives with their 2580hp Sulzer 12cyl 12LDA28-C engines, provided the mainstay of the traction units used on the former Great Eastern main line. Many of these well-kept Stratford based locomotives which had silver painted roofs, were given appropriate East Anglian names and carried a cockney sparrow logo. Here we find No. 47585 *County of Cambridgeshire* working a Norwich to London Liverpool Street service and awaiting departure from Ipswich. This locomotive was later converted to a Class 47/7 and became 47757 *Restitution. (NF)*

Ipswich engine shed or motive power depot was located at the south end of Ipswich Tunnel and approximately 69 miles from London Liverpool Street. The shed was rebuilt in 1954, with closure to steam traction officially taking place in 1959 although steam locomotives could still be seen there in 1960. This view shows various Type 2 diesel locomotives and one Drewry Car Co. 204hp diesel shunter at the depot. (*MWC*)

A fine late 1940s scene showing Class B1 4-6-0 No. 61043 of Norwich shed on an express near Halifax Junction, the location of Ipswich water troughs. Designed by Edward Thomson and introduced in 1942, locomotives of this type were the last steam engines to work under British Railways at several East Anglian locations when used for the steam heating of rolling stock in the mid 1960s. (*DWC*)

Resplendent in LNER Green livery at Colchester on 10th August 1933, Class B12/3 4-6-0 No. 8580 was a Gresley rebuild, introduced in 1932, of the S. D. Holden design of 1911. For many years the B12s were used on heavy express trains on the Great Eastern Railway network and indeed continued to perform well on the London to Great Yarmouth and Lowestoft fast trains well into the 1950s, in addition to working services on the former M&GN to Yarmouth Beach. This locomotive was scrapped at Stratford during April 1959 but one of these impressive machines, No. 61572, is preserved and is based on the North Norfolk Railway. (LH)

The Class J15 0-6-0 is another steam locomotive type now preserved and based on the North Norfolk Railway. Allocated to Cambridge shed, J15 No. 65475, is seen here out of use adjacent to Colchester shed. (DW)

The Class WD 2-8-0 was introduced in 1943 having been built to a Ministry of Supply design. After the end of the Second World War, many were acquired by the LNER in December 1946 for heavy goods work across their network. These were numbered 3000-3199 in the LNER numbering scheme. Large numbers of additional locomotives of this type were acquired by British Railways in 1948-49. An example of the Class WD 2-8-0 is seen here at Colchester shed in August 1951. In 1947, one of this class LNER No. 3152, was fitted with an oil burner and became the subject of much attention. It worked in East Anglia on a number of occasions(FC)

Another Colchester shed scene from 1951, showing a visitor from Cambridge shed in the form of J. Holden Great Eastern designed Class E4 2-4-0 No. 62784. Fitted with a side window cab, No. 62784 had probably worked in with a Cambridge train. Locomotives of this type were frequently seen on the East Suffolk line. (FC)

An unusual view from the Ipswich end of Colchester station with Britannia Class 7MT 4-6-2 No. 70040 *Clive of India* approaching with an up express. The train is approaching the 40 mph speed restriction which was in force prior to alterations to the track and rebuilding of the platforms at Colchester. At the time this scene was recorded *Clive of India* was a Norwich engine. Two of this impressive class, No. 70000 *Britannia* and No. 70013 *Oliver Cromwell* are preserved. On the left are the sheds, where Class B1 4-6-0 No. 61054 , a Class J19 and two Class B17s can be seen. (*GM*)

Introduced in June 1950 to provide a fast service to Great Yarmouth and Lowestoft from London, "The Easterling" was scheduled to run non-stop between Liverpool Street and Beccles, where the train divided, one section going to Lowestoft, and the other to Yarmouth. Class B1 4-6-0 No. 61234 worked the down train on the morning of 29th July 1950, and is seen here near Kelevdon. The overall time for the journey between the capital and the coastal resorts was less than 3 hours. (*LCGB/KN*)

No. 61670 *City of London* was one of the two Class B17 locomotives streamlined in the late 1930s to coincide with the introduction of a special train, "The East Anglian". The locomotive was classified as a B17/5 as a result of these changes. In April 1951 the streamlining was removed and *City of London* was reclassified as a B17/6. Earlier identities carried by this locomotive were LNER No. 2870 *Manchester City* and No. 2870 *Tottenham Hotspur*. No. 61670 was withdrawn from service at Lowestoft in April 1960. The streamlined *City of London* is seen here on 2nd October 1948 with the 8.00am Yarmouth South Town - London Liverpool Street express near Chelmsford. (*LCGB/KN*)

For many years Lowestoft's Class K3 2-6-0s worked the fast fish trains between Lowestoft and the capital. One of these locomotives, No. 61959 was kept in pristine condition by the regular crew of Driver George Freeman and Fireman Alfred Hubbard. No. 61959 is seen at Goodmayes, which is 9 miles 23 chains from London Liverpool Street, in the early 1950s.

Above Left-Driver George Freeman with No. 61959 ready to return to Lowestoft. Note the superb condition of the locomotive. (*AHC*)
Above Right-In the cab on the left is Driver George Freeman and, on the right, Fireman Alfred Hubbard. Top right on the tender is the Yard Foreman, and the other four chaps are Shunters. (*AHC*)

Waiting to leave Liverpool Street for Lowestoft with the "Holiday Camps Express" is "West Country" Class 4-6-2 No. 34039 *Boscastle,* at that time on loan from the Southern Region. On the left, reversing out of the station is Britannia Class 7MT 4-6-2 No. 70003 *John Bunyan.* On arrival at Lowestoft, the "Holiday Camps Express" would be taken forward to Corton, Hopton and Gorleston by a Lowestoft engine such as a J15, J17, L1 or a Yarmouth allocated D16/3. The year is 1951. *(FC)*

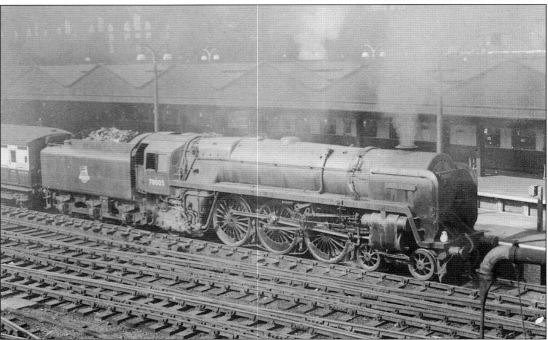

Another scene from 1951 at London Liverpool Street, but with Britannia Class 7MT 4-6-2 No. 70005 *John Milton* about to depart with an express to Norwich. The fastest start to stop time in the 1950s for the Britannia locomotives, was in the Ipswich to Norwich section which was 46.3 miles in 44 minutes (63.1 mph). This was by the 9.30 am, 12.30, 3.30 and 6.30 pm from Liverpool Street. In the other direction, the average speed over the same section was 61.7 mph, again achieved by four trains. The fastest pass to pass timing was 72.8 mph between Haughley and Tivetshall. In the late 1950s, Liverpool Street with 18 platforms, was handling an average of 174,600 passengers per day. *(FC)*

South Lynn-Yarmouth Beach

Designed by Johnson and built by Sharp Stewart, the M&GN Class C 4-4-0s were introduced in 1896 and subjected to a series of rebuilds and modifications spanning many years. Rebuilt class member No. 53 is seen here with a Midland G7 boiler which it was fitted with in 1910, a Midland firebox and short chimney. No. 53 was withdrawn from from service in 1940. The Midland & Great Northern Joint Railway (M&GN) was formed in July 1893. *(MWC)*

Well situated for the locals and popular with holidaymakers, Caister-on-Sea station was one of the better supported small stations on the M&GN main line and justified through and express trains from London and the Midlands stopping there. Like many others on the line, it opened on 7th August 1877 and closed on 28th February 1959. An interesting passenger's view of the station is captured in this 1958 scene. *(StationsUK)*

Leaving Yarmouth on the former M&GN route and after passing Newtown Halt, the next station/halt was Caister-on-Sea. Situated on the approach to the station was this distant signal. The beach is on the right of the photograph and quite close to the track at this point. (*MWC*)

Seven halts, very basic platform structures with few if any facilities, existed to the north of Great Yarmouth on the former M&GN route. This distant signal was located in the vicinity of the halt at California. (*MWC*)

One of the attractive features of the former M&GN was the splendid scenery the line passed through. At Caister-on-Sea the line ventured close to the beach and seashore where we find Class 4MT 2-6-0 No. 43160 heading the 16.50pm Yarmouth Beach-North Walsham service on a sunny day in April 1957. (EA/CR)

Recorded on 6th August 1923, M&GN Class C 4-4-0 No. 14 is seen running into Great Ormesby with a Melton Constable to Yarmouth Beach train. Great Ormesby station was 5½ miles from Yarmouth Beach and situated between California Halt and Hemsby. (LCGB/KN)

An evening or late afternoon portrait of Great Ormesby in 1949. The station opened in August 1877 and closed with the line on 28th February 1959, after which it became a private residence. Originally with single track, in 1894 the track was doubled to allow trains to pass. *(StationsUK)*

For many years a traditional boating centre, Potter Heigham station was a popular and important destination for those spending their holidays on the waters of the Norfolk Broads. The station was in many ways of standard M&GN design. In the early days, it was just a single platform with no passing loop. Class D16/3 4-4-0 No. 62517 leaves Potter Heigham in August 1958, with a stopping train and passes a Great Yarmouth bound train in the other platform. One of the basic railway halts was located in the village nearer the river.*(FC)*

In contrast to the previous scenes of a busy and apparently vital rail and transport link, all was to change for this direct route between the midlands, Great Yarmouth and at one time Lowestoft, when closure was announced on 12th July 1958 and carried out on 28th February 1959. Many found it hard to believe that at a stroke, this previously major route, could be removed from the railway map. Some believed the line had been starved of traffic by diverting it to other lines in order to make the line unprofitable. All was not completely lost and although not any longer at Stalham, the station building there managed to survive and eventually passed into preservation on the North Norfolk Railway, after being dismantled at Stalham, and reassembled at Holt. After closure, track was removed in some locations with great haste, in particular between Yarmouth Beach and Aylsham. Railway land was also quickly acquired by new owners for redevelopment, especially between Yarmouth and Caister. Large sections of former trackbed are now in use as a road between Stalham and Potter Heigham.
Stalham is seen here after the contractors had removed the track, but almost everything else still appears in place, waiting for the trains that would never come again. (*EDPpics*)

Ivatt LMS Class 4MT 2-6-0 No. 43160 is seen at Potter Heigham with a train for Yarmouth Beach in 1958. This locomotive was allocated to Yarmouth Beach shed at the time. Originally a class consisting of 162 locomotives, one of these efficient and flexible locomotives, No. 43106 is preserved. (*FC*)

Opening on 13th June 1881, North Walsham Town station was situated close to the GER North Walsham Main station and located 86¼ miles from Peterborough North. The station had a large goods yard which handled coal, bricks, sugar beet, timber and also farm animals to and from the market in the town. The station closed on 28th February 1959, although some goods traffic continued to be handled in the yard for a while after closure via a short spur off the Norwich - Cromer line, at the south end of the Main station. Today much of the station area is in use as a road, as is the trackbed to the southeast of North Walsham. (*StationsUK*)

Melton Constable was very much the centre of activities of the Midland & Great Northern Joint Railway. Although losing much of the previously important engineering work during the days of the LNER and British Railways, it continued as an important junction with lines leaving the town for the east, west, north and south. With closure of most of the former M&GN lines on 28th February 1959, the station lost the important through traffic from the midlands to the East Coast.

A J. Holden GER designed Class J17 0-6-0, a type introduced in 1901, arrives at Melton Constable with a goods train in 1957. (FC)

Melton Constable engine sheds on 5th May 1957 with Ivatt 4MT 2-6-0 No. 43146 and Hunslet 0-6-0 diesel mechanical shunter No. 11172 on shed. Both were allocated to Melton Constable at the time. (MWC)

Going back to 1934 at Melton Constable, where we find three M&GN Class A 4-4-0 locomotives awaiting their fate. Nearest the camera is No. 24, No. 22 is in the centre and No.35 at the end of the line. Withdrawal from service for No. 24 came in May 1941, and for No. 22 in 1936 with No. 35 being withdrawn the previous year. (MWC)

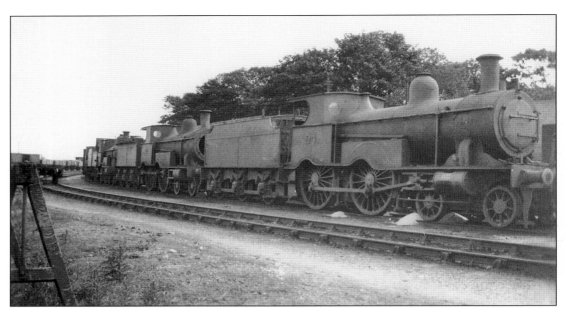

The Holden GER designed Class J17 0-6-0 locomotives were a versatile type, in addition to goods, they could often be found on heavy passenger workings. Class member No. 65551 is seen at Melton Constable on 18th August 1958. One example of this fine class, No. 65567, is preserved as part of the National Collection. (FC)

Two views recorded from almost the same location, but many years apart, of the engine sheds and other buildings at Melton Constable. The station opened on 19th January 1882 and closed on 6th April 1964, when the passenger service to Sheringham, Cromer, and Norwich Thorpe was withdrawn. This service had been maintained for a number of years using diesel multiple units.

Top - In M&GN days, with the works shunter 0-6-0ST No. 16, in the centre. This former Gt. Yarmouth & Stalham Light Railway engine was originally named *Stalham*. With the formation of the Eastern & Midlands Railway it became No. 16, which was later amended to No. 16A. *Stalham* was built in 1877 by Fox, Walker at the Atlas Engine Works, Bristol, and was finally withdrawn in 1936. Coaching stock seen here is of Great Northern Railway origin, the suppliers to the M&GN of many passenger vehicles in the 20th century. *(MWC)*

Bottom - With closure imminent, this 1959 view shows two Class 4MT 2-6-0 locomotives on shed and a Metropolitan Cammell diesel multiple unit in the station on the right. *(MWC)*

A number of towns in north Norfolk including North Walsham, Aylsham and Fakenham, had two stations. This was possibly not ecomonical or cost effective for the railway companies since the size of the local population may only have justified one station. In the case of Fakenham, the West station was provided by the M&GN, and the East station by the GER. Fakenham West station, seen here in 1958, was situated 51¼ miles from Yarmouth Beach. By the mid 1960s, both stations at Fakenham had closed. (*StationUK*)

After the closure to passenger traffic of the major part of the M&GN on 28th February 1959, a few sections continued in use. Goods trains continued to pass through Hillington until the late 1960s and it is during that era that this scene was recorded. Hillington, known as Hillington for Sandringham, was used by the Royal family on numerous occasions. (*StationsUK*)

On 21st April 1924, M&GN Class D 0-6-0 No. 62 heads a passenger train near Hardwick Road from Spalding to the Norfolk coast.
Designed by S. W. Johnson, No. 62 was built by Neilson & Co. in 1896 and withdrawn in 1939. *(LCGB/KN)*

M&GN Class C 4-4-0 No. 11 makes a fine sight as it leaves Lynn with the 1245pm to Melton Constable. This locomotive was built by Sharp, Stewart in 1894 and withdrawn in August 1942. *(LCGB/KN)*

To many, the station at South Lynn was looked upon as the gateway to East Anglia and to the railway it was an important location. Two large goods yards were to be found at South Lynn being used for the reception, holding and interchange of freight traffic from the east and west of the former M&GN.

Seen approaching South Lynn with a passenger train is Ivatt Class 4MT 2-6-0 No. 43109, one of many of that type allocated to the former M&GN lines, and in fact, a South Lynn (31D) allocated locomotive. (*FC*)

Seen passing through the station at South Lynn with a van train is Gresley designed Class J6 0-6-0 No. 64191. Built for the Great Northern Railway, these locomotives were introduced in 1911. This locomotive was allocated to New England shed in the 1950s.(*FC*)

A passenger service existed between the former GER station at Kings Lynn and the former M&GN South Lynn station. This service was provided in later years by a push-pull set, powered by a Class N7 0-6-2T locomotive. Other passenger trains including the midlands to Hunstanton through services, used the rail link from South Lynn to Kings Lynn. In this view, the train from Kings Lynn, hauled by a Class N7 locomotive approaches South Lynn station and signalbox on an overcast day in August 1958. A Class J17 0-6-0 and a London Midland Region Class 4F 0-6-0 can be seen outside the shed on the right, with a diesel shunter in the background. Introduced in 1924, the Class 4F locomotives were regular visitors to the M&GN and could often be found at Yarmouth Beach in the summer months. As with the J17, the 4F was used on passenger and goods trains. (FC)

A classical scene at South Lynn with M&GN Class A 4-4-0 No. 28 in the shed yard. Withdrawal from service for No. 28 came in February 1938. (MWC)

The engine shed at South Lynn was replaced in 1958. Ironically it would not be long before the new structure would be made redundant by the withdrawal of passenger services through the station. South Lynn opened on 1st January 1886, and closed to passenger services on 28th February 1959.

Top - The timber engine shed which was replaced in 1958. The shed had been extended in 1895 to hold 10 locomotives and in the early 1930s it was substantially modernised. In addition to J. Holden designed Class J66 0-6-0T No. 68378 on the left, other locomotives on shed include former GNR 0-6-0s, Class 4MT 2-6-0s, and former GER tender locomotives. The date is 11th May 1952. (MWC)

Bottom - The replacement engine shed with an interesting assortment of locomotives on shed, including Classes B1 4-6-0, 4MT 2-6-0, J17 0-6-0, and various former GER tender and tank locomotives. (MWC)

Abreviations

A number of abbreviations are to be found in the photographic captions, and included in these are the following:-

Anglia	Anglia Railways
BR	British Railways
EUR	Eastern Union Railway
GER	Great Eastern Railway
GNR	Great Northern Railway
HCE	Holiday Camps Express
LMS	London Midland & Scottish Railway
LNER	London & North Eastern Railway
M&GN	Midland & Great Northern Joint Railway
"one"	The present train operating company (TOC) for the majority of East Anglia rail services. It commenced operations on 1st April 2004.